For Debbie and Hugh

Irene M. Endicott

WHAT WILL YOUR LEGACY BE?

True Stories of Lives Well Lived

By Irene M. Endicott

WESTBOW
PRESS®
A DIVISION OF THOMAS NELSON
& ZONDERVAN

Scripture quotations are from the Revised Standard Version of the Bible, copyright 1946, 1952, and 1971 the Division of Christian Education of the National Council of the Churches of Christ in the United States of America. Used by permission. All rights reserved.

This book is a work of non-fiction. Unless otherwise noted, the author and the publisher make no explicit guarantees as to the accuracy of the information contained in this book and in some cases, names of people and places have been altered to protect their privacy.

WestBow Press books may be ordered through booksellers or by contacting:

WestBow Press
A Division of Thomas Nelson & Zondervan
1663 Liberty Drive
Bloomington, IN 47403
www.westbowpress.com
1 (866) 928-1240

Because of the dynamic nature of the Internet, any web addresses or links contained in this book may have changed since publication and may no longer be valid. The views expressed in this work are solely those of the author and do not necessarily reflect the views of the publisher, and the publisher hereby disclaims any responsibility for them.

Any people depicted in stock imagery provided by Thinkstock are models, and such images are being used for illustrative purposes only. Certain stock imagery © Thinkstock.

ISBN: 978-1-5127-6701-8 (hc)
ISBN: 978-1-5127-6700-1 (e)

Library of Congress Control Number: 2016921227

Printed in the United States of America.

WestBow Press rev. date: 6/20/2017

We all leave a legacy. Billy Graham will.
Margaret Thatcher did. Adolph Hitler did. So will you.
The greatest legacy of all is our finest example.
It is the life and teaching of Jesus Christ.

DEDICATION

To Lynn Harsh and Bob Williams

For trusting me with the Freedom Foundation legacy program

ACKNOWLEDGEMENTS

Special thanks to my friends, Marilyn and David Taylor for your wisdom in selection of Scriptures for this book and for your friendship. I am grateful to Juliana McMahan and Marsha Michaelis for assistance reaching important contacts for some stories; to Michael Barvick for contributing the Foreward; to Mike Reitz and Tom McCabe for your support of my work at the Freedom Foundation, for the inspiration you are to me and for giving me the opportunity to meet so many unforgettable people during my tenure as Legacy Society Director. Thank you to my colleagues at the Freedom Foundation. It is a privilege to work with you great freedom warriors. Thanks to Boaz Crawford for your expert design work on this book and to the patient staff at WestBow Press, div. of Thomas Nelson & Zondervan, I thank you. Loving thanks to my family and friends for being there for me throughout this writing. Thank you, Amy, for your courage to write about Jeremy. And to the subjects of each of the stories in this book; you touched my heart. Because of the principles and values by which you live, many more people will be moved to think about their own legacy. Thank you for sharing your life stories with us. You are examples of everything that is good about America. I will never forget you.

CONTENTS

FOREWORD

The planned giving expert Robert Sharpe often explains that success in receiving estate gifts is most often reserved to those charities that inspire donors to "elevate the organization to the status of family member." When I was asked to provide the Foreward for *What Will Your Legacy Be?* the first word that came to mind when considering Irene Endicott's legacy was 'family.' If you ever have the privilege to meet Irene I can guarantee that you'll feel like part of her family before you know it. It's what has made her a successful wife, mother, grandmother, author, media personality and champion of freedom.

Irene has been an inspiration to thousands of people during her lifetime. When I first became the Director of Planned Giving at The Heritage Foundation in Washington, D.C. I asked around about who I should consult to share best practices as I developed our own program. Irene's name continued to come up. I reached out to her and she immediately welcomed me to meet with her to share her secrets of success at the Freedom Foundation.

In *What Will Your Legacy Be?* Irene shares stories from those individuals who have become part of her extended family that have made an impact on her life. Her hope is that you will be inspired to think seriously about your own lasting relationships and the legacy you will leave. Scripture reminds us, "Where your treasure is, there your heart will be also." I'm certain after reading the stories contained in this book you'll have a new perspective on those things that are truly worthwhile as you live the journey of your own legacy.

Michael Barvick, *Director of Institutional Advancement, Oakcrest School and fmr. Director of Gift Planning, The Heritage Foundation*

INTRODUCTION

*A legacy is defined as the impact, influence or imprint we leave
in the lives of those we care about. We create
it either by purpose and intent
or we create it just by existing day by day. Every day
of life contributes to our living legacy. The product of
those many days will define the legacy we leave.*

The Legacy of Stories

We can learn from the true stories in this book and apply the basic principles from each one to our own lives. Stories are a gift to us. The telling can bring a certain peace to the teller, after decades of living the story. Stories can also be a cathartic blessing to the reader who has lived through similar circumstances; they can be confirming to those who are living meaningful lives, and inspirational to the young person who needs encouragement to become a shining example to other young people.

Stories can also be the source for understanding that, in retrospect, Almighty God was at work through thick and thin. That revelation is humbling and a tremendous learning experience for anyone who has not yet sought fellowship with Him.

In my life's work, I have been privileged to meet extraordinary people whose life stories tell of unimaginable courage, deep faith in God, astonishing physical and mental endurance, outstanding leadership and obedient stewardship of God-given resources. Their stories will touch your heart and give you a new perspective on your own precious life.

My goals in writing this book are:

1) to affirm you in your choices if you recognize and live by the principles and values in the stories;

2) to rejoice with you if, by reading these stories, you see that you can begin to make changes for good in your life and that those changes will be your legacy;

3) to help you understand that God is with you always and that He has the Plan for your life.

One couple in their 90's shared with me the story of their long lives. The interview lasted three hours. I came away emotionally drained by what I had been told. Some painful truths in the text they would not allow me to put in print.

Going back to clarify portions of the manuscript several times, I learned more about them; their sweet spirits for the Lord, their devotion to each other and their perseverance through crises that could have sabotaged the successful lives they were living. All of it was very moving.

When their story published, I called them to say thank you for the privilege of writing about them. As was their habit, both got on separate phones to talk to me. I did my best to express my gratitude and thanked them again and again for allowing me to tell their story.

Silence followed. I waited. I wondered if we had been disconnected. Then, the silence was broken by her soft voice saying, "No, we thank *you* for telling our story. *Nobody has ever asked us.*"

Kevan Kjar, author of *The ArrowHead*, teaches that one of the greatest gifts we can give another person is to listen to their story. I agree. Let us remember to try to be a willing listener. You may be the only one in that person's life who makes the effort.

"You yourselves are a letter of recommendation, written on your hearts, to be known and read by all men; and you show that you are a letter from Christ, written not with ink but with the Spirit of the living God, not on tablets of stone but on tablets of human hearts. 11Cor 3:2, 3

There is great power in the words you use as you create your legacy. Passing on God's Word can be the very essence of your gifts to heirs. Dollars to loved ones are temporary gifts. Dollars to organizations you believe in can impact for generations. The message you convey in your Last Will and Testament as a follower of Christ is eternal.

"Heaven and earth will pass away, but my words will not pass away."
Mt: 24,35 RSV

Legacies are made in many ways, sometimes simply by the way we live our lives every day, leaving an enduring legacy of love, kindness, fun, strength of character, working, providing, saving, sharing, teaching, learning, cooking, playing.

Legacies come from living a life of faith, from patriotism or great accomplishments in business, sports, academia, or public service. They are made by our response to circumstances beyond our control. Parents and grandparents can also pass on wisdom learned through victories and trials.

Be inspired by the following exemplary legacies of lives well lived and take some time to consider what your legacy will be.

Here is a list of principles and values you may recognize from the stories told in this book:

VALUES AND PRINCIPLES

- Peace
- Joy
- Faith
- Intellectual Growth
- Service
- Authenticity
- Thoughtfulness
- Family
- Commitment
- Freedom/Liberty
- Work Ethic
- Loyalty
- Spiritual Development
- Trust
- Integrity
- Generosity
- Hope
- Compassion
- Perseverance
- Forgiveness
- Humility

- Justice
- Honor
- Love
- Fairness
- Truth
- Wisdom
- Power/Influence
- Consistency
- Honesty
- Modesty
- Gratitude
- Courage
- Confidence
- Financial Security
- Responsibility
- Frugality
- Respect
- Optimism
- Faithful Prayer
- Creativity
- Risk

Other: _____

_____

WHAT WILL YOUR LEGACY BE?

KATHERINE AND MEL NESTEBY

WHAT WILL YOUR LEGACY BE?

THE POWER OF FAITH

Duty. Honor. Country. These words were etched in the very soul of Mel Nesteby, U. S. Infantry soldier, who survived the 1941 Bataan Death March and four prisoner of war camps during World War II.

Mel enlisted in the Army in May 1941. He was assigned to the 31st Infantry Regiment in the Philippines. Mel said the unit was at half strength, about 2,000 men. When war broke out December 7th, he had received most of his basic training and, being a strong man and the tallest in his platoon, was assigned the Browning automatic rifle, 30 caliber, as his weapon "to balance the fire power of the platoon."

In a speech given July 28, 1999, Mel shared his experience as an infantry soldier on the front lines at Bataan and as a prisoner of war:

"We put up a valiant effort for Bataan under the leadership of General McArthur and General Wainwright. After 105 days of skirmishes, fire fights and close combat, we were overwhelmed by the sheer number of fresh enemy troops brought in from Singapore. We had fought the original Japanese forces to a standstill, but at that time, we were out of food, water and medical supplies and I was sick with malaria and dysentery. Combat losses were severe. Most of the officers were casualties. We gave it all that was humanly possible.

"When the Japanese troops broke through the last main defense line at Mt. Sumat, the infantry shock troops we needed did not come. We were the walking dead. Colonel Jones, a West Point infantry officer, could see that further combat action would be fruitless. He took a white flag and went forward to the enemy lines and surrendered the Bataan Peninsula. Our flag came down. I was wounded. And we all faced a death march.

"I was in four Japanese prisoner of war camps, placed first in hospital #1 until Corregidor surrendered. My first encounter with my captors came as they entered the hospital area with fixed bayonets. They immediately took any valuables they could see. They took my watch, my ring and a small bag of personal items. We complied in order to stay alive. Some hours later, they came back to the ward tent, demanding everyone get up and out! Those who could not get onto their feet, and there were many who could not, were rolled to the ground by tipping the cots over.

"I grabbed my makeshift crutch, made from a four and a half foot bamboo pole with a tee shirt wound around the top for padding. I got upright and hobbled outside to join men with wounds of every description and we were herded down a trail toward the main road. After one mile, I was falling behind. I expected to be shot, but it didn't happen. I made it to the next camp.

"Every day of the many months in that camp was a life and death struggle. Food furnished to us consisted of cooked rice, about three cups per day, or about 750 calories. I was forced to join a work detail every day. When my clothes disintegrated, I was furnished a used Japanese army uniform. When my shoes wore out, I was given sandals. I slept on bare planks with one blanket. Most of the guards were hostile, using every excuse to hit us with their walking stick or to slap us.

"Heavy artillery guns were placed right next to the hospital tents and were fired relentlessly at Corregidor. After three more weeks of Japanese artillery fire of more than 1,000 rounds per day, Corregidor surrendered as a large enemy combat force landed on its beaches.

"Some days after that, I was ordered onto a truck and taken to an old Spanish prison called Billibid in the city of Manila for six months. It was a dungeon beyond description. Then to twelve months in the infamous Cabanatuan camp. We were subjected to physical and mental torture, given weevil-infested rice and forced to work every day. Many, many died there. I was then taken in the ship, Maru Nagota, to Hari Hata Camp B-12 for twenty four months in captivity."

Mel spoke emotionally about the day he was liberated in 1945; "One day the Japanese guards opened the prison gates and marched out. We were all walking dead men, and watched in a daze as, for the first time, they left the gate wide open and disappeared down the road. The realization that indeed we were free came slowly. I feared they would come back. Two days later, the American troops arrived and my dearest hope became reality."

He was free! At six feet tall, Mel weighed 117 pounds.

It took four long years for him to recover from injuries and illnesses he suffered during the war and as a POW. Amazingly, in 1951, he re-enlisted in the Army, served one year in the Korean War and was on Occupation duty in West Germany for three years during the Cold War for a total of nine years of overseas duty. He was awarded the Purple Heart with three Oak Leaf Clusters; two Bronze Stars; three Presidential Citations; The Combat Infantry Badge and seventeen other medals.

Although Mel never fully recovered, he never complained, greeting each day with joy and happiness because he was a free man. He loved America and our flag.

After the war, the Surgeon General of the United States gave a report to Congress and the President on the Bataan POWs, including his opinion that there was no human reason the POWs survived.

Mel said he survived because of his Bible. Following is a synopsis of an essay Mel wrote:

My Bible

My Bible and I were in all 50 states and 12 foreign countries during my 21 years of service to my country. It was my closest companion, friend and counselor. Its words and message are etched in my heart forever and ever.

We traveled together to the Philippine Islands. When Pearl Harbor came about, I was given battle gear and placed my little Bible in my shirt pocket, close to my heart. I felt super strong with it there, as though the hand of Providence was directing me.

My Bible was with me at Bataan when we were completely surrounded by enemy foot troops and our options were to surrender or die. We tried to stall the offensive war machine from taking over Bataan. Alas, we could not. My Bible was taken from me when I was wounded.

Some 18 months later, I was lying on my plank bed, recovering from a malaria attack when a voice asked if I was Mel Nesteby. He said, "I have something for you" and laid something in my hand. It was my long-lost Bible! My heart leaped with joy! To me, that was a true miracle. I told a fellow prisoner about it. He told me that my Bible was found in the camp in the Zero Ward where prisoners were taken and left to die. Hundreds and hundreds had their final moments holding my Bible.

My Bible stayed with me as I boarded the Japanese ship to Japan to a prisoner of war camp. In the two long years there, I kept my Bible hidden in a rafter overhead and feared all the time that it would be taken from me again.

My Bible and I witnessed the Hiroshima bomb drop, just 33 miles away, the surrender of the Japanese government, the Japanese troops surrendering the POW camp, and the rickety train ride to Yokohama, Japan where we were processed back into U.S. control.

Then came that wonderful trip home, and passing under the Golden Gate Bridge.

My Bible was with me during a four-year struggle to regain my health. My Bible and I have seen the best and the worst of mankind during 42 months as a prisoner of war. Only God knows the truth of the brutality and deprivation of which I can scarcely speak.

Mel's Bible

Mel's small Bible (the New Testament) was donated to The Army Historical Foundation. It is tattered and broken in places, but revered as a Divine instrument in one man's survival of unspeakable trials, and by the grace of God.

I visited with Mel for the last time in 2009. At the end of the interview, he stood, still tall and exuding confidence. We walked to the door. Mel stood straight, laid his long arms across my shoulders and looked down at me with a purpose. He had a farewell message for me.

This faithful servant who loved his country and loved God whose Word sustained him through the agony of almost four years as a prisoner of war, then made him well again, said this:

"Love the Lord with all your heart and never, never allow an enemy to take away your freedom. Stand strong for all that you believe and all that you know to be true."

Mel passed away May 16, 2009, two months shy of his 89th birthday. He is buried at Arlington National Cemetery.

Lincoln Bennett, a WWII Navy veteran, says this about his dear friend: "I had the greatest respect for Melvin Nesteby. In all the years I knew him, he never displayed anger about his terms as a prisoner of war. He considered his time in the military as the obligation of an American citizen to do his duty. He was always polite, kind and helpful to everyone he met."

> *"Light rises in the darkness for the upright; the Lord is gracious, merciful and righteous."* Ps 112.4 RSV

What principles and values from this story are also foundational in your life?

From Mel: _____

_____

ALVIN AND CAROLE STARKENBURG

A LEGACY OF STEWARDSHIP

> "The circle of life is bigger than yourself. It involves work, family, relationships, and charity. You make the choices on how your circle is completed. That is your legacy."
>
> *Alvin and Carole Starkenburg*

The Circle of Life

The Starkenburg family had its beginning in Whatcom County near the Canadian border. Alvin was born in Sumas, Washington where he attended Ebenezer, a little country grade school with a class of eight students. He later graduated from Lynden Christian High School. Carole graduated from Lynden Public School right next door. They met at the Christian Reformed Church in Lynden and were married there 54 years ago. The family home is situated on three picturesque acres. Their four children and 19 grandchildren all live in or close to Lynden.

Theirs is a loving family with traditional values of strong faith, rewarding work, patriotism and giving back.

Alvin is a living example of those values. He worked in construction after high school, saved his money and at age 19, bought a trucking company, hauling hay from Eastern to Western

9

Washington. Four years later, he started the S & W Sand and Gravel Company which became a major force in its industry, including site development, road building and land development.

He tells us, "When we went into the compost business, ours was the first North American plant for the W.L. Gore Company solid waste division. We call it Green Earth Technology or G.E.T. The environmentalists didn't like us as sand and gravel people. We went into composting and now they think we're the best! Both of our companies function side by side."

Alvin is still working for the company at age 73. He and his daughter, Stephanie are co-owners now and different grandchildren have worked summers. Grandson Caleb was working for the company until his deployment to Iraq in July of 2015.

The Circle of Family

As the businesses grew, the family has also grown. Carole cherishes her role as mother and grandmother. "Alvin and I find reasons to get together with our girls - Patty, Lesa, Stephanie and Amy. That is important. Our grandchildren are growing up! Five are being home-schooled, one is in private school and two are in public school with many activities. Two more are away at college and several are living at home, commuting to college and the rest live close by.

"On the Fourth of July, we stage an Olympic-style family event. We divide into teams to compete in a wide variety of events, making it very competitive with high incentives to win like additions to college savings, money for a trip or something else we know they really want. We have everything on the property for our own Olympic challenges, including go carts and an indoor swimming pool and we have a wonderful time!"

Thirty family members competed last year, ranging from the youngest grandson at age 7 to Alvin's age. As always, they had a memorable time.

Carole is passionate about her family. She says, "In today's pop culture, we have to support our kids, morally and spiritually. In some public school districts, kids are not getting properly educated in reading, writing and arithmetic. There is too much emphasis on feelings and political correctness. What ever happened to achievement and accountability?"

Carole is also pro-life. She served on her local Pregnancy Resource Board and commented that "it's tough when another organization gets all the money and you are struggling to get one ultra-sound machine."

The Circle of Relationships

The Starkenburg's principled commitment to family is mirrored by rock solid relationships built in other circles of their life together. These relationships are with conservative organizations that promote the Constitution and belief in the values and principles of America's Founders.

The Circle of Charity

One relationship dear to their hearts is with KidsTown, International, a mission the Starkenburg's have supported for 15 years. KTI serves more than 500 needy children in 25 locations in Romania, India and Nepal.

Alvin says, "We pooled resources with our friends, John and Gladys VanBoven, of Lynden and together we support one orphanage in Kathmandu, Nepal - the House of Hope. It is amazing to see how God has blessed this effort; from nothing in a land with so much poverty, to a place where 23 little girls, age three to nine, thrive in a wonderful home with dedicated house parents where they receive an education that includes drama and music! Our experiences as we have visited over the years overwhelm our hearts with gratitude and joy!"

Carole adds, "A time-consuming part of the mission work is consistently writing to the girls to let them know we care about them. A wonderful women's group called Coffee Break at Bethel Church in Lynden took on this task. They write encouraging letters and send Christmas cards to each one."

The Starkenburg's also support the Cedar Springs Christian Retreat Center which was started in Sumas more than thirty years ago. With great emotion, Alvin says, "When you live in freedom with every opportunity to succeed, it is important to give back. Most mission work is not done by famous celebrities, but by ordinary people like us."

Living Beyond Our Own Circle

Alvin says, "You have to be concerned about things that have changed over time in our state and country. They are still happening. For example, environmental matters: it's one regulation after another. My dad had a 140-acre dairy farm. We worked so hard as kids to get the land productive. Over 40 or 50 years, it's all gone back to nature – by regulation. It's not producing a thing today. The punitive effect over the years was huge. We lived it 'on the ground.'

"I am so disappointed in our leaders. They have had many opportunities but they have not stepped up to the challenge of leadership. Government is supposed to be for the people. It is sad that a lot of voters either don't care or are not interested in whether our leaders know the Constitution. But even though you might be disappointed in our state and national leadership, don't let failed expectations turn into discouragement. There is hope in all of this. Bad leadership causes good leaders to step forward. God is still in control."

Carole adds, "We can't just sit back and trust. We have to get involved and not get discouraged. Discouragement is a choice. In your life, a Higher Power is at work. Never doubt that."

> *"Lead me in thy truth, and teach me, for thou art the God of my salvation; for thee I wait all the day long. Ps 25.5 RSV*

What principles and values from this story are also foundational in your life?

From Alvin _____

_____

From Carole _____

_____

TERRIE O'NEAL AND MR. LONGANECKER

Photo: Jeff Rhodes

WHAT WILL YOUR LEGACY BE?

WISDOM FROM THE ZOO

Terrie O'Neal owns a small farm in Snohomish, Washington which has been dubbed by her neighbors as "The Hillside Zoo." A sign on the porch says *All the Animals – Two by Two.*

Terrie's mission is caretaker, feeder and vet to the animals who stray onto her property looking for a "soft touch." At the Zoo, many of them find love and compassion for the first time.

There are two dogs, Dooley and Mr. O'Toole, and two pygmy goats, Cricket and Clair.

A burro named Prancer joined the others. Prancer loves to dance. When he arrived, Terrie says he watched the other animals sort of dance around so he tried it and liked it. He lifts his legs proudly and cocks his head from side to side. There is a clearly visible, natural Christian cross on his back. That means he is a descendant of the burro that carried Jesus. Prancer can also unscrew the light bulb in the shed.

There's a gander named Mr. Longanecker who came with a friend. She became Mrs. Longanecker. Three hens live at the Zoo. One is named Grama Nubby, the second is named OH! because she walks around the barnyard saying "OH!- OH!" And third is BB, named for the initials of a dear friend.

Mow Mow is the refugee cat, a Brindel who arrived in very poor condition; moth- eaten and starving. She has gained five pounds. Mow Mow is a good mouser. Mr. Brinkley, the rooster came to live at the Zoo when he was just a chick. Friends who had him roosting at night at the bottom of their bed with papers on the floor brought him over assuring Terrie that he was tame as could be. Terrie thought, "Oh sure. Until he sees the hens!"

Mr. Brinkley has grown considerably. He likes to drill Terrie's legs, and anybody else's legs he can find, with his spurs. Mr. Longanecker runs interference and protects Terrie. He chases Mr. Brinkley away, usually pulling out some of the rooster's iridescent green and blue tail feathers in the process. Terrie says, "I'm convinced that the Good Lord made roosters drop-dead handsome to compensate for the fact that they are dumber than rocks. This one struts around the barnyard crowing "I'm drop-dead handsome!"

Three new rescued goats are Penelope; a calico; Lola; and her baby, named Eve because she was born on Christmas Eve. Also new on the property is Newky Mow, named by Terrie's two-year-old grandson who had trouble saying New Kitty. But he could say Mow, for the other cat, so he put the two names together and the new cat's name became Newky Mow.

Newky Mow arrived with his left eye slit from top to bottom and badly infected. For him, Terrie called in a professional vet who thought the injury came from a fight with another cat. Terrie puts drops in Newky Mow's eye faithfully every day. The vet is amazed that Newky Mow allows Terrie to put drops in because many cats would complain. Newky Mow lifts his chin up to receive the medication when he sees Terrie coming. He's getting better day by day.

They come to the Hillside Zoo and they stay. Terrie says, "You never know what the Lord is going to send tomorrow. My dad always cautioned me, quoting Exodus 23:20, to be careful because you might be entertaining angels. He sends his angels in different looking suits!"

The gate to the Zoo is known to neighbors as the place to check to see what's going on in conservative public policy circles. Terrie posts important messages there from time to time for passersby to see. She alerts neighbors and guests to pending elections and reminds them of their civic duty to vote. She posts newspaper articles, sometimes enlarging the type for easier reading. She places them on cardboard and in plastic against the weather.

Terrie says people need to know what is going on in their state and in their country, especially the younger ones! She has this advice:

"Some of the young people in my life were raised in Christian conservative homes, but as they have grown up a little, they have learned that prayer isn't welcome in school in America anymore and that the Constitution is a living document to be changed at a whim and in college they are literally being brainwashed! They don't think their one little voice is going to be heard by government. The truth is that one voice joins another and another and before you know it, you have an army! That's what is happening right now in America!

"We have to reach out to young people through the written word and through social media. That's where they live. Just walk down the street or into a restaurant anywhere or even in a church service in America and you will see kids and grown-ups alike staring at their phone screens. If they are walking, sometimes they run into you! Some kids are missing out on actually talking with family and friends.

"Machines are replacing the art of conversation. They don't have to think anymore. All the answers are on the Internet. They aren't learning how to solve problems. Kids only have time today for what's on their computer and that's the way to get to them!"

Terrie thinks our kids are really like her animal friends on the property. "They need love," she says. "They need direction, discipline and a personal touch from a caregiver like a parent, or a friend and they need to feel like they belong. Otherwise, they won't ever reach their God-given potential."

The goose and the gander are the longest time residents at the Zoo. Mrs. Longanecker's favorite place on the property was the creek in the lower pasture. Terrie noticed she hadn't been moving very well for a few days. Then one day she was missing!

Searching every nook and cranny, Terrie walked down to the creek and there lay Mrs. Longanecker. She had simply gotten old and Terrie thinks she made her way to her favorite place, had a swim, laid down by the creek and died. She says, "Mrs. Longanecker returned to her Maker. I rejoice because I know that she knew she was loved."

Now, missing her, Mr. Longanecker goes into the coop with the hens. Terrie says, "The girls make a terrible racket and force him out, but he'll try it again."

As the only human at the Zoo, Terrie does everything herself, from first light to dusk. She says, "It's up to me to keep order, take care of everybody and I leave the rest to God."

> *"And God made the beasts of the earth according to their kinds...*
> *and everything that creeps upon the ground according to its kind.*
> *And God saw that it was good."* Gen 1.25 RSV

What principles and values from this story are also foundational in your life?

From Terrie: _____

From the animals _____

BOB AND JANE WILLIAMS

Photo: Boaz Crawford

WHAT WILL YOUR LEGACY BE?

A LEGACY OF INTEGRITY

Bob Williams was born at home in Mt. Carmel, PA. Tragedy struck when Bob was nine months old. His father was killed in a car accident. His mother, widowed at age 24 with four children, could not afford to raise him, his brother and two sisters.

At age eight, Bob and his brother were sent to a school for fatherless boys in Philadelphia – Girard College, where he lived and studied from third grade to twelfth grade and graduated. Bob says Girard was the best thing that could have happened to him.

"I learned how to focus and work hard. I learned the Golden Rule and acquired a deep faith in God. I put my finger in the crack of the actual Liberty Bell in Philadelphia and have never forgotten the patriotic lessons I learned."

Bob's after school jobs included working on a soda pop truck where his pay was as much pop as he could drink; a bakery truck with pay being as much day-old bakery goods as he could eat; and working on an ice truck for a block of ice for his icebox.

One day, selling magazines, young Bob knocked on the door of a man who asked him some questions, then expressed delight, saying that he also had graduated from Girard!

Mr. Pete Wambach was married and a father of 13. He became a father figure to Bob, treating him as his 14th child. He gave Bob a vision for college which led to acceptance to Penn State University in 1959. Mr. Wambach helped him get scholarships. Pete was an influential democrat.

Bob says, "He was a great man – a millionaire who gave it all away to help others. I don't know what might have become of me without Pete. He taught me a good work ethic and introduced me to some politicians, including the governor of Pennsylvania!"

At Penn State, Bob was the leader of a conservative student group. In 1961, he led a successful boycott of a barber shop because the owner refused haircuts to blacks.

He earned a Bachelor of Science degree in business and accounting and was a member of ROTC. On graduation day, he was commissioned into the Regular Army as a Second Lieutenant and ordered to active duty in Ft. Knox, Kentucky prior to attending officer's training.

Bob served in the United States Army from 1963 to 1968. In Nuremburg, Germany in 1965, he met his life partner, Jane Hanson, who was working as an Army civilian in Special Services. Jane was born and raised in Tacoma, Washington, and graduated from the University of Puget Sound. After a year of teaching, she took a job with the Army as a recreation specialist. She was sent to Nuremberg, Germany where she planned games, local tours and managed birthday and other parties for enlisted soldiers. Jane shares this charming story:

"In 1965, I was engaged to another fellow in Germany. I met Bob on a cold October night when a soldier asked me to deliver a cup of coffee to his Lieutenant who was on guard duty. Bob occasionally stopped by the enlisted men's club for a visit.

"That spring, he happened to be on the same ten-day tour of the Holy Land that I was scheduled for. I noticed that Bob was a little bit chummy with me. I thought, as an engaged woman, this wasn't proper. I was chilly toward him. Unbeknownst to me, Bob got down on his knees on that tour and prayed, 'Lord, I just don't think Jane is engaged to the right person. Would you find her someone else?'

"Three days later, it was my 25th birthday. Bob arranged for 64 little cakes, one for each person on the tour, with my name on each cake. He approached my table and said, 'Let's announce our engagement.' We had never dated! I had only seen him at the post! I looked at him a moment and said, 'Well, all right.'

"I broke up with the other fellow. The only picture I had of Bob was with a turban on his head, sitting on a camel, looking perfectly ridiculous. My mother thought I had lost my mind. God gave me a love for Bob. We were engaged in March and married in July 51 years ago. It was the Lord's Will."

Assigned to Ft. Lee, the couple moved to Virginia. After retirement, Bob took a job as an auditor at the Government Accountability Office. (GAO) They later settled in Tacoma, Washington where Bob worked for Weyerhaeuser Company as a financial analyst.

Still wanting to serve his country, Bob ran for the Washington State Legislature where he served for 10 years from 1978 to 1988.

"I term-limited myself at ten years. After I left the House, I was encouraged by many to run for Governor. The Lord didn't tell me I would win. He told me to run. Through several miracles, money came in, amazing friends helped us. We waged an honest, hard hitting campaign but someone else prevailed."

In 1991, with Lynn Harsh, a highly respected conservative teacher, Bob founded Evergreen Freedom Foundation, a public policy organization, in Lynn's basement with a faithful, all-volunteer staff. The rest is history.

Twenty six years later, their hard work has impacted state government for good. The Foundation's mission is to advance individual liberty, free enterprise, and limited, accountable government. The organization gained a state and national reputation in education, budgeting, property rights, voter integrity and teacher paycheck protection.

Renamed Freedom Foundation in 2009, a new and highly successful mission has been added; courteously educating the members of SEIU (Service Employees International Union), a government union, that the United States Supreme Court passed a law in 2014 that SEIU forgot to tell their members; that it is now illegal for the union to deduct money from home care workers' Medicaid reimbursement checks every month for purposes and candidates they do not support. The effort is spreading across the country under the direction of CEO Tom McCabe as better informed government union members opt out of union membership if they wish.

Bob is now a Senior Fellow at the Freedom Foundation. Not ready to retire, he founded State Budget Solutions, working with governors and legislators who are willing to make a difference by advancing sound budget principles and reforming the pension system. SBS is now part of the American Legislative Exchange Council (ALEC.)

Throughout his long career of public service, Bob says, "I couldn't have done anything without Jane. She had to be mom, dad, chauffeur, disciplinarian, cook – everything! She is great!"

Bob and Jane

Photo: Boaz Crawford

Bob's dedication to his state and country is motivated by a deep faith in God and the basic principles of freedom and liberty. To better understand the depth of Bob Williams' commitment, here is a portion of his testimony, given in 2007, which reads as if it was written for today:

"Today, like Ezra of old, nearly two generations of Americans don't really value the Scriptures. Many have never studied God's Word and tens of thousands sit in churches today for only the social value of coming together or belonging. They have forgotten about the redemptive and restorative work of God.

"The roots of America are spiritual. If a tree loses its roots, it withers and dies and produces no more fruit. Likewise, with nations, if we lose our life-giving contact with our spiritual roots, we will cease to exist as a nation.

"It is time to restore decency, financial accountability and integrity to America. We must start in our corner of the world, where God has placed us.

"We must remember that freedom is not free. Liberty does not come without a price.

"Where else but in America could a kid like me have the freedom and liberty to go where I have gone, meet the people I have met and done what I have done? Each one of us needs to try now to make a difference for freedom by being passionate about keeping the America God gave us or we are going to lose it!"

> *"According to the grace of God given to me, like a skilled master builder I laid a foundation and another man is building upon it. Let each man take care how he builds upon it. For no other foundation can anyone lay than that which is laid, which is Jesus Christ."* I Cor 3.10,11 RSV

What principles and values from this story are also foundational in your life?

From Bob _____

_____

From Jane _____

_____

DR. JOHN AND CARRIE VASKO

Photo: Joel Sorrell

WHAT WILL YOUR LEGACY BE?

THE SUCCESSFUL LIFE

"Our Constitution is designed only for a moral and religious people. It is wholly inadequate for any other." John Adams

D r. John and Carrie Vasko's story is about having goals and realizing your dreams, even if it takes an eternity. John is a respected physician, now retired. He divides his time between home, music, politics and church.

Carrie is the daughter of a former Washington state governor, a homemaker and teacher, who today, is pursuing her lifelong passion for child evangelism. This devoted couple followed the career paths laid out for them. Today in retirement, they are having the time of their lives!

The son of an orthopedic surgeon, John was born in Great Falls, Montana in 1934. His father was in the Army Reserve just before the declaration of World War II. He was activated and stationed at Ft. Lewis, so the family moved to Tacoma. John's seventh birthday party was December 7, 1941.

John recalls, "Some birthday celebration that was! When the attack on Pearl Harbor was announced, the ladies wept. It was a sad, frightening time for everybody. Dad was sent to Pearl Harbor and our family escaped the drizzly rain of Tacoma and moved to Fresno, California."

After the war, the family moved to the San Francisco Bay Area. John graduated in 1960 with a biology degree from Stanford University in 1956 and received his medical degree from the State University of New York, Downstate Medical Center.

During his training, in 1958, John's parents came to New York to attend a medical convention and took John out to dinner, along with good friends visiting from Spokane, Washington. That evening, John learned about two young ladies from the Northwest who were working there in New York. The Spokane couple gave John their phone numbers. He put them in his pocket and forgot about them.

One of the numbers belonged to Carrie Ellen Langlie, the beautiful daughter of former Washington state Governor Arthur B. Langlie, who served one term, then served in the Navy and was elected again, making him the only chief executive of the state elected to three terms. Carrie's home for twelve years was the governor's mansion in Olympia. In 1958, her father accepted the presidency of a national magazine publishing firm in New York and moved the family there.

Carrie had graduated from the University of Washington in 1957, where she hosted a radio show called *Guests of America;* interviews with international students. In New York, she worked for NBC Monitor radio, assisting the producer of comedy vignettes starring Bob & Ray, Jonathan Winters, Milton Berle and others. She says, "I had all the fun!"

John finally got around to calling Carrie Ellen. A perfect match, they dated and were married in 1959. After medical school, the couple headed back to Seattle for John's internship at King County Harborview Hospital. Their son, John Arthur, was born in July of 1960. Second son, Christopher Louis, followed in 1962. By this time, John was in surgery residency in Oakland, California, at the same hospital where his father had interned thirty-five years before.

John joined the Air Force, serving as a Captain at Vandenberg Air Force Base from 1962-1964. He decided to change his medical specialty to radiology and moved to Ohio State University where he continued his training and says. "I found radiology fascinating and served with several fine groups of physicians in the Seattle area until my retirement in 2005."

John also developed a serious interest in public policy back in 1964. When the family settled in Seattle in 1974, John became a precinct committee officer. He served as chairman of the King County Platform and Rules Committee several times and has been a delegate to the Republican Convention every year since 1978. He says, "I like the issues aspect of politics, but I don't mind doing some of the 'grunt work.'"

While practicing radiology, John also led Bible studies, enrolled at Fuller Seminary for a year and was a church Elder for twenty years. Reflecting recently on the issues of today, John spoke with conviction about the future of America, saying, "Rome failed. We're following the same general path. Unless we can recover the faith that underlies a working Republic, we are going to fail, too. If we don't have a revival of the very core and character of the Christian faith in America, it's over.

"I believe that revival has to have serious intellectual substance. God revealed Himself in the Scriptures, but also in different ways to Aristotle, Plato, Aurelius, Cicero, and Augustine. I think our founding fathers believed that. They knew the Scriptures, but they also knew those writings, along with Smith, Locke and Montesquieu. There is a lot of truth there - truth that influenced what they came up with in our original political system."

Carrie says her strong faith has grounded her. "I like to work as a support person. I thank my dad for the principles he taught me. He was responsible first to God, then family, then in service to others.

"Life for us has not always been easy. I needed those principles and my faith in a mighty way a few years ago, when we lost our son, Christopher, in a drowning accident."

The list of organizations supported by this dedicated couple is long. John says, "I like organizations that *do* things like file lawsuits, write demand letters and use cutting-edge communications technology to an extent that is really pioneering and effective."

In retirement, the Vasko's are realizing their dreams. John has played piano since the age of four. He was so captivated by baroque music that he built a harpsichord that stands in the foyer of their home. He took up oboe four years ago and plays with the Eastside Symphony Orchestra. John is thrilled that several of their eight grandchildren also love and play music.

Carrie continues teaching Bible to children and serving in support roles when asked. Carrie has one major goal left – one dream that only God can fulfill. With tears of joy, she tells us what it is: "Lord, help me be your servant, that one day, You might say, 'Well done, thou good and faithful servant.'"

John adds, "Part of my e-mail address is *Boanerges*, derived from the Gospel of Mark, 3:14-17 which says, 'And he ordained the twelve. Simon he surnamed Peter; James, the son of Zebedee, and John, the brother of James, he surnamed *Boanerges*, translated as '*The Sons of Thunder.*'"

John and Carrie's generous philanthropy to organizations is helping to protect the Constitution and make our country better. They inspire all of us that whatever our goals and dreams may be, one day, they can come true.

> *"For the Lord gives wisdom; from his mouth come knowledge and understanding; he stores up sound wisdom for the upright; he is a shield for those who walk in integrity."* Prov 2.6,7 RSV

What principles and values from this story are also foundational in your life?

From John _____

_____

From Carrie _____

_____

ED AND EMILY LESFERD

Photo: Joel Sorrell

WHAT WILL YOUR LEGACY BE?

A LEGACY OF IMMIGRANT CHILDREN

Fifteen year-old Stanley Lesferd stood, shivering on the pier at New York Harbor, his pockets as empty as his stomach. He was just off the ship from a long, arduous trip to America, the land of freedom and opportunity. It was 1905.

The boy waited in the lines, poor as a church mouse, certainly questioning what might happen and whether the promise of freedom was really true. He had fled his homeland, a part of old Russia, now Poland. There was no hope for a future there. He longed to be free!

This immigrant was Ed Lesferd's father. Stanley's is a story of sacrifice and grit in a quest to achieve the American Dream. And achieve it he did!

Walking the streets of New York, young Stanley took the only job available to him; the worst job in a slaughterhouse. He got to work on time. His strong work ethic spurred his determination to do his very best. Stanley was rewarded with promotion after promotion. Eventually, he left to become the proprietor of his own meat company. He married, raised a family and invested his money wisely. But this is a story about his son, Ed, who saw his father's sacrifices and determination firsthand growing up in Rome, New York in 1920.

With passion, Ed reflects, "As a kid, I watched my father go to work every day and get home late and do it all over again day after day. He had a strong will to succeed. He came from poverty to become a successful American business owner. I wanted to be like him."

Ed worked many jobs as a boy and saved his money. "When I was nine years old," he says, "I knew I wanted to go to college. So, after high school, I took my savings to Catholic University of America in Washington, D.C. I had saved $1,000 which was the cost of tuition, room and board in the 1930's. Working myself through school, I earned a Chemical Engineering Degree in 1942."

Ed couldn't get a job in his chosen field because employers knew he would be eligible for the draft. He got his notice and enlisted in the Army Air Corps which was advertising for meteorologists. It wasn't chemical engineering, but he signed up and was sent to the Massachusetts Institute of Technology (MIT) for training as a weather forecaster.

Little did he know where that training would take him.

———————

Meanwhile, a pretty little girl named Emily was growing up in Boston, Massachusetts in a home environment that almost defies belief. Emily's mother immigrated to America from Germany, bringing with her an obsessive loyalty to Nazi Germany and Adolph Hitler.

She married quickly. Emily was born with brown hair. Her two brothers were blonde which fit the Nazi quest for an all-Aryan Race. She talks about feeling like she was shrinking within herself as she watched her brothers being smothered with their mother's love and attention, leaving Emily an outcast in her own family.

Emily confides the pain of her youth, growing up in America as the daughter of an immigrant Nazi mother:

"My two brothers were fair and blonde. I was the only child with brown hair. When I refused to salute Adolph Hitler each evening, raising my arm high and saying 'Hiel Hitler!' I was put outside in the cold in just the dress I was wearing and my brothers ate my dinner. I got my face slapped regularly and was loudly berated in front of my brothers. One day, the FBI came to our home with a search warrant and confiscated my mother's shortwave radio. That was very frightening for me."

Her voice rising with a mix of anger and sorrow, Emily remembers, "I was ignored day after day in my own home! I was shunned for not being Aryan. When I was four, my mother took me and my two brothers to Germany. She told us it was for a brief visit. We stayed two and a half years. I had to go to school in Germany."

Survival in her family was a daily battle. When Emily was ten years old, her father lost his job. He died of cancer six years later as the family spiraled downhill, living on welfare until Emily graduated from high school. Life at home continued to be dominated by her mother's loyalty to Nazi Germany and Adolph Hitler.

Emily went to work as a very young girl. Her mother confiscated every penny of her earnings at the front door when she came home. Her mother screamed at her often that she needed to get married and get out. Emily withstood the indignities of her home life with a steel spine. Today, what happened to her would be prosecuted as "child abuse."

"Growing up, my mother taught us that Germany won World War I," Emily confides. "When I got further along in school back in America, I read that America had won that war. I confronted my mother, who shrugged it off, saying "Germany *should* have won it!"

Emily was determined to survive and be her own person, vowing many times as a child that when she grew up, she would never, never be poor. She took small jobs, then, after high school, went to work in a factory, "working like a man," she said. "It was very hard." Then she got a job at Metropolitan Life Insurance Company in the office and that was better.

The war came in 1941. Emily wanted to do her part so she joined the United States Coast Guard in 1944. She was promoted three times, discharged in 1948 with the rank equivalent to an Army sergeant and enrolled at Long Island University in New York on the G.I. Bill.

Emily attacked her studies! Driven by her vow that she would never be poor, she earned a Bachelor of Science degree in Business Administration in two short years, cramming in credits per quarter, four quarters per year – all the while working part time and maintaining a required B average.

Jobs were scarce on the East Coast in 1949, so she and a girlfriend moved to Seattle. Emily attended the University of Washington, where she earned a Master's degree in Librarianship.

During those tragic early years of Emily's life, Ed Lesferd had been fighting his own battles and winning. After completing his Army Air Corps meteorological training at MIT, Ed was commissioned in September of 1943 and a few months later, found himself part of the biggest convoy of WWII, heading for Europe in February of 1944.

Ed chronicles what he calls his "small part" in the effort:

"There were 11 ships plus cruisers and another 13 ships joined us out of New York," he remembers. "It was the invasion and we were on our way to Europe. I was tapped to join the 9th Air Force Bomber Command where most of the Air Force mission weather forecasting was done for bombing raids. I was just a 23-year-old Second Lieutenant with the job of gathering data for the senior forecaster who would then report the forecast to the commanding general who decided to send or not send the planes up.

"Today," Ed says, "forecasting weather is easy because of terrific technological advances. We had none of those helps. During WWII, you had to be an artist to draw pictures describing the weather.

"June came and there was a lot of sudden activity. We knew something was up when they painted all the wings of the bombers with a stripe so they could distinguish American from German planes. The weather was hit and miss much of the time as data was often scarce. Fog was our biggest challenge. We made intelligent guesses, played the percentages, tossed a leaf in the air to test the wind and prayed.

"The troops moved quickly across France. The 9th Air Force had only smaller bombers such as the B-25 and A-20. We moved with the troops."

It is painful for Ed to recall the fighters or bombers that took off – piloted by young men like himself - and hearing later about the planes coming back, badly shot up, some with one wing. He laments those that didn't make it back at all.

Following the Invasion, headquarters was relocated to Chartes, France and a few months later, to Reims and finally to Namur, Belgium until the end of the war.

Discharged April 1946 as Captain, 21st Weather Squadron, United States Army Air Force, Ed went to work for Northwest Airlines in New York. In 1949, he came to Seattle, Washington to begin a 29-year career with the Boeing Company as a computer programmer.

In 1950, the lives of these two children of immigrant parents converged in Seattle when Ed met and married the pretty little girl from Boston. Emily continued a teaching career and retired as a librarian in 1990. Ed invested his money wisely, just as his father had done. They have one daughter, Cynthia, and two grandsons.

Candidly, Ed says, "We worry about our grandsons' futures with what is happening in our great country today. We are active politically and do our part. We need leadership badly!"

Ed and Emily spend their retirement years working in the gardens at their beautiful home in the Northwest and they travel the world.

Emily in her rose garden

Photo: Joel Sorrell

Ed says, "I think of my father often and the great example he was to me. He passed away at age 83. We are deeply grateful for the opportunities that America has afforded us – to be FREE to strive for the American Dream, share our good fortune with others less fortunate and support those organizations that defend our freedoms."

At this writing, Ed has celebrated his 96th birthday and is in fine spirits. Emily is approaching her 100th year, currently residing in a nursing home, after being returned there for the third time from hospice care.

As she has done all of her life, Emily refuses to give up.

"I press on toward the goal, for the prize of the upward call of God in Christ Jesus." Phil 3.14 RSV

What principles and values from this story are also foundational in your life?

From Stanley _____

From Ed _____

From Emily _____

MASATO DAVID YOSHIMATSU

WHAT WILL YOUR LEGACY BE?

BELOVED SON

The letter arrived out of the blue at the Schmidt home. It was ten pages, handwritten in impeccable English, postmarked March 1988, Tokyo, Japan. It was a mother's plea for her son, Masato David Yoshimatsu, who attended a heavily regimented Japanese school where he wasn't flourishing. She thought he would do better in an American school and asked please that David come to live with the Schmidt family in America where he could be free and study.

For fourteen years, Howard and Norma Schmidt had taken foreign students into their home in Bellevue, Washington to help them achieve their academic goals. Each student attended either the International Business program at Bellevue Community College or Sammamish High School where Howard taught history for thirty-four years before retiring.

Of the four Schmidt children, Brent and Braxton were grown and on their own. Brandon and Annaliese were still living at home, so Howard and Norma asked them "What do you think? Should we take him?" They said yes and Brandon added, "It will keep you young, Mom and Dad! David can have my room!"

Howard wrote back to the mother, listing ten conditions to taking David into their home – ten mandatory conditions to which he thought the mother would never agree. Shortly, another letter came. Mother had agreed to all ten conditions and asked for a date they might arrive a few days before school was to start.

In August, David arrived at the Schmidt home with his mother who inspected the room where her son would live. Saschi, whose Christian name is Sarah, earned a Masters degree in English from the University of South Carolina and is a professor of English in Japan. David's father, Hidemi, is a television executive. They are members of the Anglican Church in Tokyo and travel extensively.

Mother approved David's living arrangements and departed for Japan.

So began the American experience for Masato David Yoshimatsu.

Howard and Norma delighted in David almost immediately. The boy was curious about everything and questioned everything in excellent English. He was eager to learn and consistently sought out a wide variety of experiences in America.

A typical teen, David required discipline from time to time. There were the fads, long hair, and he learned some slang. Rather than come down too hard on him, Howard and Norma asked for peer counseling for David from Annaliese and Brandon. It worked!

David thrived. He achieved good grades in school and made many friends. During the summer of 1989, along with a French teacher and her husband, Bonnie and Greg Brodd, Howard took fifteen students on a five-week trip from Paris - on the 200th anniversary of the French Revolution - to the Island of Crete. Along the way, David was afforded leadership opportunities and a new confidence in himself and his abilities emerged.

He developed a very close relationship with Brandon Schmidt, who had played soccer at Sammamish and was recruited to a national soccer camp. Brandon had been voted the most inspirational player on his high school soccer team three years in a row and for an additional three years on the championship team at Santa Clara University. Howard told his son, Brandon, that of all of his soccer trophies, he was proudest of the most inspirational player awards he had received.

David was in awe of Brandon's achievements and accompanied the Schmidt's to a number of his games at Santa Clara. He tried to emulate Brandon but was not strong physically. He turned out for soccer and didn't make the team. He turned out for swimming and made the team but never placed in any meet. But he was always there to encourage and inspire his team members to victory.

In his senior year, David received the most inspirational player award. Knowing the background, when the award was announced, there were more than a few proud tears shed by the Schmidt family. For David, it was one of the most affirming acknowledgments he had received in his young life.

His academic achievements soared steadily in his three years at Sammamish under the watchful eye of his American host. Howard Schmidt is a highly regarded Austrian School economist who believes that American history cannot be taught without also teaching an understanding of economics and free markets. He is well known as a demanding teacher who expects the best from his students.

David took Howard's class in his senior year, always sitting in the back of the room. He received no special favors, no tips on exam questions at home. He did the work.

That class was a turning point. David didn't earn an A from his tough teacher, but he approached Howard one evening at home to say, "I want to go to college here in the U.S. where they teach what you teach."

Saschi and Hidemi approved the idea. David applied to Hillsdale College, Grove City College and George Mason University. Joy abounded in the Schmidt household when the letter of acceptance came from Hillsdale College.

Saschi arrived at the Schmidt home that summer of 1990. She and David loaded up his belongings in an older Volkswagen they had purchased for him, said farewell to the Schmidt's and mother and son began a harrowing adventure across the country, from Washington State to Michigan that included flat tires and other car trouble. They arrived at Hillsdale with many stories to tell.

Mother went back to Japan and David settled into his new environment.

David was the only Japanese student on campus and was instantly accepted. He drew friends with his sense of humor, his personality and his writing ability. He majored in economics and studied German, the original language of the Austrian free market scholars. He wrote a regular economics column in the Hillsdale student paper. His future goals became clear. He achieved a 3.5 grade average at the demanding school and looked forward to earning a Ph.D in economics and becoming a teacher.

The Schmidt's welcomed David back home for a seven-day spring vacation in 1993, after which he went back to Japan, thinking of little else but finishing school and moving on with his future. He accepted a summer job at a Tokyo department store.

On July 13, 1993, Saschi went in to wake David for work.

He did not wake up. He would never wake up again.

Their beloved and only son had passed away during the night. An aneurism had stolen David's promising future.

Saschi called Howard and Norma immediately, hysterical with grief. The Schmidt's, stricken with shock and disbelief, could scarcely comprehend what they were told. The previous week, they had congratulated David on his 21st birthday.

With heavy hearts, the Schmidt's could not travel to attend the memorial service at the Anglican Church in Tokyo. But Howard's reflections on that spring of 1993 when David spent those precious vacation days with them were a cathartic blessing for him. While he was there, David had made special calls to all of his Sammamish High School friends and visited with many of them. Then he went back to Japan to be with his parents following his sophomore year.

To Howard, it seemed as though David had said goodbye to all of them.

Hillsdale College invited the Yoshimatsu's to a special memorial program that fall as students came back to school. David would have graduated in 1995. Howard and Norma traveled in June of 1995 to the Hillsdale graduation ceremonies where Saschi and Hidemi Yoshimatsu were presented the degree that David would have earned.

Hidemi accepted the degree, held it tightly in his hands with tears streaming down his face.

Hillsdale professor, Dr. Richard Ebeling, now a Visiting Professor of Economics at Trinity College in Hartford, Connecticut, and his wife, Anna, invited the Yoshimatsu's and the Schmidt's to their home for a special student recognition social after the ceremony.

In an interview, Professor Ebeling said, "David came to learn about the ideas and ideals of freedom and the free society. His untimely death occurred just a few months before he was to take his first economics class with me at Hillsdale. I had many opportunities to interact with a young man who clearly had a burning passion for liberty and a keen mind, already thinking about markets and economic freedom. Our talks revealed that he both understood and mastered what he had read and he was enthusiastically awaiting the start of more advanced courses.

"It is clear to me that a wonderful, active mind was cut short by his death. I am absolutely certain that David would not only have performed brilliantly in the rest of his undergraduate education, but would have gotten through a graduate program in economics and gone on to a uniquely contributing career. Economics and the cause of freedom lost a most promising young individual far too soon."

David had lived in a dorm at Hillsdale. Students gathered money and a tree was planted by his window - a David Crabapple with flowers that appear every spring. The plaque says, "In Memory of Masato David Yoshimatsu."

The cherished bond of friendship deepened over the years between the Yoshimatsu's and the Schmidt's. Both Saschi and Hidemi came to Brandon's commencement exercises in May 2000 when he received an MBA at the University of Michigan. When Brandon was married in a mission church in Santa Clara, Saschi came from Japan, dressed in formal kimono for the ceremony. When Brandon's first son was born, Saschi sent a little Japanese baseball suit. The Yoshimatsu's, the Schmidt's, including their sons, Braxton and Brandon and his wife Shannon were hosted at a Hillsdale luncheon in May 2000.

Irene M. Endicott

The families are connected forever by the memory of their beloved son.

Sadly, Howard says, "We continue our long friendship with David's parents. We all miss that fine young man so very much. We mourn him and we know Sarah and Hidemi will mourn him forever."

David would have taught and written in the Austrian economic model and in the style of greats such as Von Mises or Hayek. Today, other outstanding young scholars are taking up the torch of liberty, learning, then teaching others how to stand for the free market system of government and freedom as David surely would have done.

> "Assuring freedom to the free, we shall nobly save the last best hope of earth; the way is plain which if followed, the world will forever applaud and God will forever bless."
> *Abraham Lincoln January 26, 1863*

What principles and values from this story are also foundational in your life?

From the Schmidt family _____

_____

From David's parents _____

_____

From David _____

_____

WHAT WILL YOUR LEGACY BE?

PICKING UP THE TORCH

Photos by Joel Sorrell

A dults can feel helpless to make a difference in a young person's life. They may fear rejection or rebellion in their attempts to set a young person on a path to fulfillment, even greatness. So, how can it be done? Living what we preach is a good beginning, and openly talking with youngsters about any mistakes we have made, how we faced them and assuring them that they can do that, too, no matter the circumstances.

Someone took the time to influence young people who became the inspirational leaders we admire. Someone instilled in them the values and principles that changed their lives forever. Faith in God, perseverance and love had to play huge roles in the outcomes.

We worry about our children today. I suggest we lay that concern at the foot of The Cross and come alongside the children in your life, with wisdom, counsel, consistency and honesty. In today's politically correct environment of revisionist thinking and false heroes, our children need prayer more than ever.

Parents have the awesome opportunity to mold their children's lives to become all that they can be. Here is proof as told by six young college students who were accepted as summer interns by the Freedom Foundation. They personify a new generation that is picking up the torch for freedom and liberty, having received good guidance from good examples in their young lives. They give us hope for the future.

Before leaving their summer job to go back to college, the interns gave these answers to my question, *"Has someone inspired you to be who you are today and how is that affecting your future goals?"*

Bryan: My dad has inspired me. He teaches economics. Because of him, I ended up at Hillsdale College with a goal of teaching economics. I was also inspired by Dr. Wolfram at Hillsdale because he has such energy for explaining it and is very straightforward with common sense that kind of wakes people up to the truth.

Honestly, I think it all goes back to Hayek. Through his writing of *Road to Serfdom* and other things he has done, he has been able to reach so many people and turn the tide of public opinion. His work is timeless. The influence of all of these great people has helped me decide to go to grad school and actually teach economics as opposed to going into business or something like that. The influence of my dad has completely focused me on my career choice and I am so grateful to him.

Kerry: The person who has inspired me greatly and set me on this path is my father. He always told me that he was born a conservative and that he thinks I was, too. He consistently instilled in me that our country is great, and that our free market, capitalist values are worth keeping because that is how we will remain free. He talks to me about things from a conservative perspective, countering the always liberal agenda I get on the news and in school. He makes it clear to me that we should respect our military and he has taught me the importance of personal responsibility whether it is a simple thing like what we eat or what we spend our money on.

My dad is … well, my dad is frugal. He is very careful with money. He has a hard time getting a good car. He will go from place to place and end up saying he is not going to buy from them. He goes to an independent seller to buy his car. My dad has taught me so much about individual responsibility, fairness and freedom. He is the one who has set me on the path I travel today.

Efrain: I am the youngest of three children. Two people have inspired me. My oldest sister, Billenna is the first in our family to graduate from college. Growing up, she was like a savior to me. We were raised by a single mother who is the other person in my life who inspired me. She pushed me. She wanted us to finish high school, without question. College was pushed even harder. My mother is American, my father Puerto Rican. My father moved back to Puerto Rico when I was seven but always kept in touch. I was born in Fayetteville, North Carolina, but have visited Puerto Rico several times. My father is a big influence in my life as well.

Growing up was sometimes hard. We worked all the time. I was seven, helping to renovate old mobile homes, clean and paint them and place new carpeting. I did what I had to do and learned a strong work ethic.

My sister, Billenna inspired me without saying anything. She led by example really. Just being herself made her such a great human being – a great sister. We love her unconditionally and have always looked up to her. We had a lot of hard times growing up in a single parent home. Now that I am older, I can look back and see how difficult it must have been for my mother to raise us on her own. At the time, I didn't understand and had some resentment, but now

I see that she did what she had to do to put her children through a private Christian academy and a four-year university. That took a lot of sacrifice on her behalf. I say to her, 'Thank you, Momma!

Ben: My father inspired me more than anyone else to achieve as much as I could. He didn't have the same opportunities that I did and always told me what he had learned and how much I am blessed to be able to strive. That inspired me to work as hard as I could to capitalize on the opportunities he had given me and what he had sacrificed in order for me to go on. What that means to me now is not even as much as it will mean to me in the future.

Other people have influenced me also; professors, such as Dr. Wolfram at Hillsdale and the president of our college, Dr. Larry Arnn. The ideas and principles they stand for go far beyond the time in which we are living, beyond this political time and really apply to every area of our lives. It keeps me going to know that those things will still be true. They are worth fighting for and I will pass them on to my children one day.

My parents sacrificed so much for me. I am – I am overwhelmed with gratitude and thankfulness. Without their direction and guidance to help me discover my talents and strengths, I'd be pretty scared right now. I am deeply grateful.

Anna: My parents, from a very young age, gave me the ability to think; to evaluate public opinion and compare that to what I think of as important and know to be true. My dad had me listening to conservative talk radio and discussing issues from age 12. Just that start plus a commitment to doing something about what you believe, because you know it's right, inspired me. I think that really defines me right now and what drives me going forward.

There are things I am really passionate about, things that get me all riled up and make me want to shout and spread the word and make a difference. That drive wouldn't be there if it weren't for my parents. They taught me the principles upon which to live my life and showed me how to live it with passion. That is a very powerful thing and I just hope I can keep that going.

I greatly admire passionate and effective people. The leadership here at the Freedom Foundation has modeled so many ways for me to be more effective such as having the courage to stand up and talk to strangers, to say what you believe in. I want to be able to inspire others to action like that. I am an entrepreneur, through and through. I like coming up with ideas. I want to start a business.

This summer, the political arena is back in my options. In high school, I got really, really irritated with what was going on in politics and needed some place to put that energy. Back then, I just kind of blocked it out, living happily in a bubble. But at Hillsdale and now with this experience at the Freedom Foundation, I am thinking more about that. I have learned so much from this great summer internship. Very inspiring. The future will be exciting!"

Olivia: For me, it would definitely be both of my parents who inspired me in a lot of ways. My dad feels strongly that we need young people in America who are thinking about what's going on and can communicate clearly. He was my debate coach in high school and teaches debate now, working with kids, training them how to think and to be able to speak persuasively about issues. Having his example helps me to remember not to take things on face value, not to listen just to what other people say, but to come up with ideas and answers and communicate them graciously. We can't beat someone else down, speaking to them in a harsh way. We must actually speak the truth clearly and with graciousness so people can hear what we are saying. I really respect my dad for that.

Is there a young person in your life who needs you to come alongside? Whether you are a parent, friend or a teacher, you can make a difference in one life that could impact a generation and the world.

> *"...take heed... lest you forget the things which your eyes have seen, and lest they depart from your heart all the days of your life; make them known to your children and your children's children."*
>
> Deut 4.9 RSV

What principles and values from these testimonies are also foundational in your life?

From Bryan: _____

_____

From Kerry: _____

_____

From Efrain: _____

_____

From Ben: _____

_____

From Anna: _____

_____

From Olivia _____

_____

1ST LT. GEORGE GREELEY WELLS, WWII

A MARINE AND HIS FLAG

F ew events in Marine Corps history are as storied as the iconic flag raising on Mt. Suribachi during World War II's battle on Iwo Jima. The quiet event was a stark contrast to the bloody battle that claimed the lives of one third of the war's fallen Marines, later marked a deafening Allied victory and powerfully symbolized the resolve of a nation at war.

History will forever honor famed Associated Press photographer Joe Rosenthal for capturing the celebrated photo of the flag raising. But without the attention to detail of a young Marine lieutenant, this powerful image of American patriotism would likely not exist. Before that 96-inch by 56-inch version of Old Glory whipped in the wind atop the volcanic mountain in the famous photo, a 54-inch by 28-inch flag was drawn from the map case of 25 year-old 1st Lt. George Greeley Wells from Lake Forest, Illinois, the Adjutant of 2nd Battalion, 28th Marine Regiment, 5th Division.

The sharp, amiable officer known as Greeley joined the 28th Regiment shortly before the battalion began training for the Pacific campaign. After receiving orders and driving cross-country with his wife, Bobsy, and their son, Greeley, Jr., Greeley checked in with his new unit *a day late*. Noting the young officer's tardiness, Greeley's commander, Lt. Col. Chandler Johnson named him the battalion adjutant remarking, "You will be my adjutant and you will rue the day. Report on time tomorrow."

Unaware of an adjutant's responsibilities, Greeley scoured the Marine Corps manual on his new job. The document noted that an adjutant was to carry a flag. Retired Col. Dave Severance, who served alongside Greeley on Iwo Jima as Easy Company commander, recalled receiving the first briefing on the operation and being "amazed that we'd been given the mission of climbing the volcano."

Severance recalled the "young, very enthusiastic lieutenant" at the briefing, saying "When Greeley said his piece, he mentioned that the manual directed the adjutant to maintain a flag for every operation, so he took a flag from the USS Missoula and carried it in his map case. A senior officer inquired why Greeley kept a flag so close. Greeley replied, "I don't know, but I'll have it if you need it." His steadfastness helped set into action a hallmark of American history.

On the morning of February 19, 1945, following a steak and egg breakfast – their last for 35 days, Greeley recalled in his memoir: "We splashed ashore in amphibious tractors onto Iwo Jima's beaches, unable to move any closer because the beach was covered with too many Marines. We waded past our fallen brothers while braving intense mortar, sniper and machine gun fire. I made sure I had my map case. We kept moving forward and finally reached the pre-arranged command post only to realize that a well-hidden sniper was operating from two tank traps at that post. After we heard a 'ping' some of us would move forward, then we would wait for the next ping. We lived with this for a day and a half as we moved closer to the mountain.

"The first night on Iwo Jima, I spent in a foxhole with Renee Gagnon, Easy Company runner. We talked about our religious faith and he expressed no interest. I took the first watch until midnight. He took the second one. Needless to say, I was exhausted and fell into a deep sleep even though artillery and rockets were firing consistently.

"In the morning, I woke up to see Renee on his knees, praying. I said to him, 'I thought you weren't very religious.' He said to me, 'Look next to you. See that great big hunk of shrapnel? I didn't bother to wake you, but it was a tough night.' I felt blessed. We were only four hundred yards from the base of Mt. Suribachi.

"It took three days of intense fighting to secure the base. On the second day, talking to troop replacements called in as stretcher carriers for the wounded, I was shot through the arm. Fortunately, it missed the bone, so I got patched up and continued my duties. We were told later that a Marine was killed every three quarters of a minute for the first 72 hours.

"On the morning of the 4th day, Mt. Suribachi had been secured and it was time to send a patrol to the top. The colonel picked Easy Company for the job. We were very worried because we anticipated a battle going up the mountain. My colonel turned to me and said, 'Wells, do you have the flag?' We all watched the patrol of 42 men, led by Lt. Schrier of Easy Company, go up the mountain. Not a shot was fired! The troops found a piece of pipe, fastened the flag to it and raised it between some rocks. The Japanese, seeing the flag raised, suddenly threw out some hand grenades and an officer with a broken sword came charging out of a cave. He was shot. We secured the cave opening. This was the first Japanese soil taken by Americans and the first American flag raised on Japanese homeland.

"Secretary of the Navy Forrestal landed on the beach, saw the flag and sent congratulations to the battalion saying, 'I'd like that flag as a souvenir.' Colonel Johnson, who was a feisty individual, said "this is our flag. We have fought and died for it." He sent a man to pick up a larger flag to replace the initial one plus another small one for Forrestal.

"The second, larger flag was taken up to the top by Easy Company runner, Renee Gagnon."

Greeley completed his Marine Corps service as a Captain in November 1957. He moved his family to the quaint community of Harding Township, New Jersey. There, he co-founded G.W. Bromley & Company, mapping out cityscapes for local governments, long before computers were invented. He later sold the successful business to the Sandborn Map Company and became its president.

Over his years in Harding Township, Greeley sat on the city council, planning commission and eventually served as the mayor and police commissioner. He didn't speak openly with his family about Iwo Jima until years later. In the 1990's and early 2000's, he was interviewed for James Bradley's best-selling book *Flags of Our Fathers* and on *War Stories with Oliver North,* an award-winning television series on Fox News.

Oliver North said of Greeley, "The definition of a hero is not the one who catches the touchdown in the end zone; it's the person who puts himself at risk for the benefit of others. That was Greeley; humble and selfless. He may not have been large in stature, but he was a giant of a man."

Greeley on the 242ⁿᵈ anniversary of the USMC

The Marines who fought on Iwo Jima get together every five years for a reunion in Washington, D.C. They started with about 1,700 men but their numbers are dwindling as the veterans reach their ninth decade and beyond.

In the decades after the war, Greeley answered invitations from all over the country to speak about his experiences in World War II. On one of his lectures in Washington D.C., Greeley recalled the instructor reminding him in clear terms that the 300 students he was about to talk to were young, inexperienced 17 and 18-year-olds. Greeley looked out at the sea of young faces and it dawned on him that these kids were the same ages as many he served with during the war. At the end of his inspirational speech, he said, "You must remember this. When you are offered a job to do, know that you can do it because I have seen you do it!"

Greeley and his wife moved to Washington State in the early 2000's, joining their daughter, Barbara Wells Kenney, in the city of Bellevue.

Succeeding his beloved wife of 68 years, Bobsy, Greeley passed away peacefully in his sleep at age 94 on September 22, 2014.

A celebration of his life was held in October 2014 where his admirers and loved ones remembered a man devoted to family, country and the Corps. Major Sung Kim, commanding officer of Marine Corps Recruiting Station Seattle, attended the ceremony on behalf of the 35th Commandant of the Marine Corps, General James Amos.

Addressing Greeley's four children, Kim read letters from the general which said, in part: "Your dad was not only an outstanding Marine. He was also the one who provided the flag for the most iconic image in Corps' history. He witnessed the meaning of 'uncommon valor' firsthand and Marines serving around the world today are proud to carry on the legacy he helped forge. His service will forever be an integral piece of our heritage and we are truly grateful for everything he has done for his fellow Marines through the years."

Greeley Wells was a member of America's Greatest Generation. His name is etched into history for his role on Iwo Jima. His legacy will be forever remembered and honored by a thankful nation.

> *"It doesn't take a hero to order men into battle. It takes a hero to be one of those men who goes into battle." H. Norman Schwarzkopf*

What principles and values from this story are also foundational in your life?

From Greeley _____

_____

YVONNE CONWAY

Photo by Phillip Conway

WHAT WILL YOUR LEGACY BE?

FILLING A NEED

Long before beauty salons, good Samaritans traveled to homes and farms to clean, cut and curl hair. The barter system was widely used for payment and traveling was done by foot, horse and buggy and, later on, the Model T Ford. In 1983, Yvonne Conway, of Olympia, Washington brought back this helpful service and has been blessing residents in nursing homes and others who are ill, disabled, in wheelchair or bed for the last 30 years!

Her mission is to help them feel and look beautiful and to bring a little sunshine into every home she enters. She calls it *Yvonne's Mobile Hair and Beauty Service.* Her business card says: "For those confined to home, office or jail!" Her personality and sense of humor play a huge role in her career.

Along with enough equipment to shampoo, blow dry, cut or style, Yvonne brings a big smile and a gentle touch to those who may be missing that in their life. For many of her clients, having her come is an experience – an event - that they otherwise would not have.

Yvonne had spent two decades helping her husband, Phillip, in his business, which was suffering in an economic downturn. So, in 1983, at mid-life, she decided to help out by becoming a professional hair stylist.

After a brush up course on her earlier cosmetology training, she took a job in a commercial salon. It was short-lived. Things did not go well.

She lamented, "It was terrible! The girls in the salon were very young. They chattered all the time! We had nothing in common. The music was so loud I couldn't hear myself think and one day, I just went home!"

As she drove home, Yvonne remembered that when she was a girl, her mother, a dedicated nursing home visitor, spoke about the many residents who are lonely and can't get out to have their hair done and how nice it would be for someone to take the beauty shop to them and to other people who can't leave their homes.

Yvonne says, "Phillip met me in the driveway and I started in. I told him I quit! I told him I want to bless the less fortunate and create my own salon service and drive to my clients that can't drive to me, make them feel beautiful and lift their spirits. I went on and on like that for a while. My husband of 61 years was a dear, dear man. He listened to me rant, was quiet until I calmed down, then said in his patient way, 'Okay, let's do it!' Phillip's motto was also service to others."

Her devoted husband removed the back seat of her car to make room for things. Yvonne purchased the equipment she would need and that would fit in the back of her car, including a special vinyl shampoo basin for in-bed head washing and rinsing that she designed and eventually patented. The unique, deep, inflatable tray comfortably cushions the head, neck and shoulders. An attached drain hose conveniently removed suds and water into a pail to be discarded. She had a portable hair dryer she set up for residents in a seated position and a hand-held dryer for bedridden clients.

Business was good. Things went well for six years when a serious threat to the survival of her small business came in the form of House Bill 1136 put forth in the 1990 Washington State Legislature, designed to regulate the beauty service industry. The bill stated that cosmetologists may work in a licensed salon or shop *only*, which would have made her mobile service illegal.

Yvonne immediately began actively lobbying against the bill that would put her out of business, contacting every member of the House and Senate. She found agreement from many of them. Then

Senator Linda Smith took the lead and asked Yvonne to help draft an amendment to the bill that allowed for *mobile* beauty service.

Yvonne kept leaving courteous reminder messages for the legislators and more than 60 of her clients called the Hotline in support of the amendment that "allows licensed personal service operators to provide beauty services at locations other than salons for the client's convenience." The bill passed both Houses with the amendment and her business prospered.

When Yvonne reached the age of 78, she stopped taking new clients. Her son, Craig, also a licensed hairdresser, took over many of her clients and expanded the mobile service to families. Her husband and best friend, Phillip became very ill and passed away. Now, at age 80, Yvonne will retire completely.

Asked what she liked best about her 30 years with her traveling beauty business, Yvonne was quick to smile and say, "Without a doubt, it was the faces of dear people who were simply getting old and had limited mobility. Those smiles and the little notes that I've received over the years I will keep forever. They mean a lot to me."

Here is a note from a daughter: "Yvonne – you were a bright light in Mother's week. You made her feel so perky" and this one from a husband: "My wife's illness denied her pleasurable trips to the salon, but you came right to our door, suggested a new style that is easy to manage and caused my wife no pain. Thank you!"

Yvonne says, "I am just grateful that I had the opportunity to meet so many wonderful people and bring them a little happiness at a time in their lives that was often pretty bleak. It feels good to be a help to others in their time of need. And I know my mother is up in heaven with Phillip, smiling down on me."

> *"Give, and it will be given to you; good measure, pressed down, shaken together, running over, will be put into your lap. For the measure you give will be the measure you get back."* Lk 6.37-38 RSV

What principles and values from this story are also foundational in your life?

From Yvonne: _____

_____

From Phillip: _____

_____

DR. ROBERT GOETZ

Photo: Joel Sorrell

A LEGACY FOR FREEDOM

"We are progressively losing the freedom Ronald Reagan cherished. I have seen it change in my lifetime. We started in the 30's on the road to socialism." Dr. Robert Goetz

B ob Goetz was a man of science with a tender heart for his family and friends and a deep devotion to conservative principles of government. A family doctor, Bob practiced medicine for more than fifty years. He used to say, "My education is now seventy years and ongoing."

Bob's studies began in the picturesque Susquehanna River Valley in Pennsylvania where he graduated from high school and college and completed medical school at Temple University in Philadelphia in 1953. He knew his life work would be in the sciences. He was a family physician with a strong emphasis in cardiology.

While Bob was studying biology, zoology and chemistry, a gifted young woman, who had played in the band with him in junior high school, was studying music. Dorie graduated in Bob's class. They were married July 20, 1952.

Jobs as a music teacher in public school were hard to find, so Dorie landed a job as a lab technician at Temple University, Department of Pediatrics, working for the famous Dr. Victor Vaughn. Dr. Vaughn developed and perfected the exchange transfusion in newborns with Rh factor incompatibilities.

Dr. Bob said "At Temple, Dorie was looked upon with a jaundiced eye by her well-trained co-workers. After all, a music teacher working in a laboratory?" But with his chin raised high, Bob continued, "She surprised them all! Dorie applied her considerable skills to her assignment in science, and within one year, became a specialist and was greatly admired."

All three of the Goetz children inherited an interest in science. Daughter, Susan, is chief nurse at a retirement home in Spokane, Washington. Their son, Paul, retired as senior engineer at the Bremerton Naval Shipyard and daughter, Cindy, has been assistant manager in a business with fifteen employees. Bob and Dorie were very proud of their seven grandchildren.

Bob went into the Navy on the last physician's draft call of World War II, served two and one half years in active duty, but stayed in the ready reserve through the 70's, retiring with the rank of Commander. For many years, Bob taught navigation at a 90-year-old private boating education organization which has a strong emphasis on safety.

Throughout his distinguished service to his country, his teaching and his medical practice, Bob maintained a high degree of interest in governmental affairs. He was chairman of the Barry Goldwater presidential campaign for his county.

Bob says, "I provided the shoe leather and raised the money. The central committee twisted my arm to become the chair. I ran successful campaigns to elect a state Senator. As a delegate to the 1968 National Republican Convention in Miami, Florida, I listened to the great speakers, and started thinking about how precious is our way of life, about how our country got started, the original documents that ended up becoming our Constitution and I realized, even back then, that we were fast losing that. So, I became a Conservative Republican."

A great admirer of President Ronald Reagan, Bob spoke with emotion about something historian and former House Speaker, Newt Gingrich, told him.

"Gingrich said that, as a young Congressman, he was part of a group that visited President Reagan. When they stood to leave, Reagan put his hand on Newt's shoulder and said, *'I've hardly scratched the surface. Understand that what I am doing today can be soon forgotten and it will be in your hands. You've got to keep working at it and don't give up!'* Gingrich said he's never forgotten that."

Bob was a staunch financial supporter of the work of conservative organizations. On one of his many visits to Hillsdale College, he met former Reagan Attorney General Edwin Meese, who told this touching story of visiting The White House following the President's death:

First Lady Nancy Reagan ushered Meese's group into the private library where Reagan often handwrote his thoughts in pencil. He was nearly moved to tears to see the legal pads there in the library that contained three thousand subjects written about in the president's own hand. On one of the pages, Reagan wrote about watching out the window all the people going to work at daybreak: *"Where are they going? What are they doing today and how will the day be when it is over?"* The entries revealed Reagan's real feelings for ordinary citizens. His caring for people permeated his writings. Here was a President of the United States who could write volumes about the common man and also tell the leader of the Soviet Union to *"tear down this wall!"* Mr. Meese gave Bob a copy of that page which he treasured.

Bob Goetz had strong opinions about the American culture and expressed them to anyone who would listen. He said, "We are progressively losing the freedom Reagan cherished. I have seen it change in my lifetime. We started in the 30's on the road toward Socialism. I do not agree with the facade of the extreme left that call themselves 'Progressives.'"

Sadly, Dr. Bob's beloved wife, Dorie, was diagnosed with Alzheimer's Disease. Dr. Bob cared for her for six years at home, day and night, until he realized she needed to be in an institution specializing in chronic brain syndromes, saying. "She was just one mile away and they took better care of her than I could." Dorie passed away October 6, 2008.

Dr. Bob Goetz lived his adult life in the house he built for Dorie and shared with her. Their cat, *Lovie Dovie,* kept the good doctor smiling. Bob would tell visitors, "Be careful. Don't pet her or she'll go home with you." His active life of service to his fellow man continued in retirement as he volunteered his expert medical help to anyone who needed it. He would say, "More patients to see twice a week. More teaching to do. More good friends to enjoy and a country to save."

That's exactly how he lived out his exemplary life. Dr. Bob Goetz died February 19, 2016, leaving a legion of friends across the country who will always miss him.

His longtime friend, Bob Williams, co-founder of the Freedom Foundation, says, "Dr. Goetz was a great American and an inspiration to me. His legacy of doing all he could possibly do to advance the cause of freedom helped many people understand that freedom is not free and explaining, as only he could, what makes this country great."

> *"If you continue in my word, you are truly my disciples, and you will know the truth, and the truth will make you free."* Jn 8.31-32 RSV

What principles and values from this story are also foundational in your life?

From Dr. Bob _____

_____

From Dorie _____

_____

PHIL AND RUTH JAMES

Photo: Joel Sorrell

WHAT WILL YOUR LEGACY BE?

A GOOD SCOUT

"On my honor, I will do my best to do my duty to God and my country and to obey the Scout law. To help other people at all times; to keep myself physically strong, mentally awake, and morally straight."

Phil James
Eagle Scout 1933

Most boys learn the timeless values of Scouting from devoted parents who encourage and support their son to achieve the goals set before them. Not so, for Phil James. His father deserted the family when Phil was ten years old and he turned to the Scouting movement in St. Paul, Minnesota to show him the way to live or, as he puts it, how to be a man.

"Scouting took the place of a father in my life," Phil says. "It was like a lifeline and I hung onto it. I was awarded the rank of Eagle Scout in 1933. That was over seventy-five years ago and I've never been able to overcome my love for scouting."

On my honor, I will do my best

Phil applied his scout oath to his studies at the University of Minnesota, earning a Forestry degree in 1938. "It was hard to find a job at the time," he recalls. "Quite a few graduates worked for the Civilian Conservation Corps (CCC) or had to take something else out of their realm of study. I worked in social work for a few years before I met Ruth."

Ruth, a home economics graduate from the University of Minnesota, and Phil were married in St. Paul September 17, 1941. "Two months later, of course, the Japanese were stirring up the Pacific," Phil says, "and I joined the Army Air Corps aviation cadet program in Tennessee, was commissioned in 1942 and stationed in France."

To do my duty to God and my country

During World War II, Phil James flew twenty-six medium range bombing missions in a B-26 over Germany, Holland and Belgium. His targets were bridges, railroads, marshalling yards and highways. "The idea was to cut off enemy supply lines," says the pilot, "and I never got a scratch!" Phil served his country twenty-one years, leaving with the rank of Major.

In 1965, Phil met a college buddy who worked as an engineer in timber preservation for the Northern Pacific Railroad, and who said he had just hired a fellow to go to Oregon. Phil told him that if that job ever opened up again, to let him know. A year later, his buddy called and said, "Pack your bags. You're going to Oregon!"

That didn't sit well with Ruth; there were four daughters to think about, two still in school, plus the family had deep roots in Minnesota. Phil went on ahead and the family reunited in Oregon after the twins graduated from high school.

Meanwhile, Phil had started a fourteen-year career with Northern Pacific Railroad, inspecting wood products NPRR used at roadways, such as crossties, telephone poles, pilings and lumber for bridges. It was Phil's job to make sure each one met company standards and was properly treated with creosote or other preservatives to ensure longer service.

In his spare time, this dedicated flyer built two aircraft; an *RV6* which he flew for ten years and an *Avid Flyer*, which Phil built from a kit. He bought a *G18* later. Similar to the *RV6*, it was a small light plane, all metal, and a two-seater. It took off in thirty feet!

Phil took Ruth up once. He performed a snap role and didn't tell her he was going to do it. Her head went bouncing from one side of the cockpit to the other and she wanted out. Ruth smiles when she thinks of that, saying, "He's a good pilot. I'm just not a good passenger." That kind comment indicates how their marriage has lasted 67 years.

Throughout the decades of flying and working, Phil kept informed on government and was outspoken about his dissatisfaction with some state and national leadership. His concern stemmed from what he terms the loss of traditional values in America, saying, "We elect leaders and once they get the office, they look after number one. Agencies don't really want honest performance audits. They are non-elected bureaucrats! I wouldn't make a good politician."

To help other people at all times

Phil and Ruth's legacy is helping those organizations they feel are promoting their values. Their good friend and financial advisor, Bill Larson, says of this generous couple: "I've known Phil and Ruth for eighteen years and have flown with Phil in his homemade aircraft. This couple earned everything they've got. They are careful, generous givers to many organizations including their church, nonprofit organizations that promote freedom: The Fisher House, Boy Scouts of America, the University of Minnesota, Northwest Medical Teams, and Union Gospel Mission. Ruth shares Phil's love of Scouting. She was an active Girl Scout in her youth."

Second generation Eagle Scout, Bill Larson, talks fondly of his gratitude to Phil for attending the 90th birthday of Bill's Scout Troop #294. "It was my privilege at that celebration to present Phil with a unique Eagle Scout neckerchief in honor of his lifetime of service," to which Phil says, with a twinkle in his eye, "I wear it sometimes!"

To keep myself physically strong, mentally awake, and morally straight

On his morning walks, Phil still collects cans, bags of them, and turns them in for the money. At age 92, he drives other seniors who live in his building to their beauty, dental and doctor appointments at least twice a week. He says "I have to take a physical to drive and I barely got by on the last one. I stay close to home, am very careful and never drive at night."

Phil was a Precinct Committee Officer for years and has served as a volunteer at polling stations at every election for the last twenty years.

The ten-year-old boy who clung to the Boy Scout movement as a child is living a long, fruitful life that exemplifies the Oath he loves. Ruth models the roles of loving wife, mother, grandmother and great grandmother.

Through their charitable trust, the legacy of Phil and Ruth James will help to preserve for the next generation, the freedoms they cherish. Their good friend, Bill Larson, says it well: "Phil and Ruth have worked hard all their lives. They live a principled, frugal life and have never wavered from their love of country or their unselfish service to their fellow man. To me, they are the personification of what it means to be a good Scout."

> *"Listen to advice and accept instruction, that you may gain wisdom for the future."* Prov 19.20 RSV

What principles and values from this story are also foundational in your life?

From Phil: _____

_____

From Ruth: _____

_____

WHAT WILL YOUR LEGACY BE?

WEDDING OF JERRY AND KAY BUCCOLA
May 28, 1983

WEDDING OF HALEY BUCCOLA,
July 26, 2014
from left: Erik Stauffer, Katie Jo, Jill, Jerry,
Jos Frye, Haley, Kay, Jenny and Molly

A TRADITIONAL FAMILY

Today, we hear the gloomy reports from experts on the American family; that the traditional family is no longer the norm, even that it is dead. Don't believe it! Are families different today? Yes, many of them, as the culture in America has changed. Going to a Hollywood movie can have you thinking that commitment means going on a second date. Watching television you might think that most American children are born into broken homes and that young people are too busy demonstrating to worry about getting an education or a job.

But the traditional family is alive, well and thriving. My best evidence? The family of Jerry and Kay Buccola, one of the millions of traditional families in America. Here is the creed by which they live:

"Children need a married man and woman who love each other and love their children sacrificially, and with strict, consistent discipline. Without discipline in the home, parenting will be much less joyful and effective. Marriage is wonderful! Children are such a blessing! Family means everything!"

The story of this devoted couple's life together began 34 years ago when they met at a square dance. They married three months later and began a deliberate and prayerful quest for the American Dream of a loving, caring, learning and sharing family, a quest from which they have never wavered and never will because it is based on their Christian faith.

Kay graduated summa cum laude from Seattle Pacific University in linguistics and social sciences and holds Washington and Oregon teaching certificates for K-12. Jerry has a BA in Business from Cal State Long Beach and an MBA in Finance from Oregon State University. After years as a highly respected and successful real estate broker, he now owns his own real estate firm and recently, one of his five daughters joined the staff.

All five of the girls are homeschooled, bilingual, and extraordinarily gifted in music. Jerry says, "We chose to homeschool. The parenting years are so precious and so fleeting. It is a joy and a privilege to help form these lovely ladies' lives. We wouldn't want to miss a minute!"

Katie Jo, 29, is lead sonographer in cardiac ultrasound at Stanford's Lucille Packard Children's Hospital since 2009 and teaches ultrasound to Stanford University medical students. Katie Jo was born with pulmonary stenosis, an incurable heart defect which can cause major problems as the child grows. She had to have monthly EKG's and Echocardiograms (ultrasounds). Her church prayed fervently for her and she was completely healed by the time she was one year old. She is helping others to survive a crisis with which she has had real life experience. Katie Jo plays harp, piano and flute and has sung for church worship and elsewhere in the community. Two years ago, she married Erik Stauffer, a PhD microchip designer from Illinois.

Jill, 26, taught Western Civilization and English at Benjamin Franklin Classical High School in Arizona where she also coached the 7th grade boys' football team and the 9th grade girls' basketball team that placed second in the state. Jill graduated from Hillsdale College in 2013 with a BA in History. This year she studied at the University of Chicago, earning an MA in European History with emphasis in 19th century German religious education and doing all of her research in the German language. She hopes to begin PhD studies in History next year to become one of America's rare conservative History professors. Jill is currently an admissions counselor for Hillsdale College. She plays harp professionally, the piano, trumpet, French horn and sings. She served as Youth Coordinator for the

Washington State House Republican Organizational Committee with her sister, Haley in 2008.

Haley, 25, graduated from Hillsdale College in 2014 with a BA in Christian Studies. She plays the keyboard, harp, flute, guitar, sings solo and backup, and is worship director at church. President of Hillsdale College, Dr. Larry Arnn, called the *Pickled Beats*, Haley and Jill's country western band, the best band in the history of the college and flew them all back for a special show after they had graduated. They won Battle of the Bands twice and were voted best band by the student body. Church worship is Haley's passion. She was the first student in 17 years asked to conduct the Hillsdale College choir. Summer 2014, she married Josiah Frye, a mechanical engineering designer who was her debate partner when she was 14. They will present Kay and Jerry with their first grandchild this Christmas. Haley has joined her dad as an associate in his real estate firm.

Jenny, 18, plays harp professionally, plays keys and sings. All of the girls have extensive experience and high recognition in debate and speech. Jenny was ranked third in Top Speaker awards in Washington State, 14th nationally in Team Policy debating and 3rd in the nation in Humorous Interpretation. Her newest passion is Ancient History, especially Egyptian. Although still in high school, she spends hours at the University of Washington graduate library, combing through volumes on Egyptian history, culture, language and hieroglyphs. She is writing a fascinating fiction book entitled, *Joseph's Wife, the Biblical Patriarch; through the eyes of his Egyptian wife, the first of a series.* The next two books will be *Noah's Wife and Belshazzar's Wife.*

Molly, 17, won 3rd place debate speaker in the *nation* in 2016 at the national Team Policy Debate competition in Springfield, Missouri! She excels in original oratory, extemporaneous speaking and apologetics. Like her sisters, Molly plays many instruments and sings. She and Jenny recently auditioned and were selected for parts in a church musical, *A Light in the Attic.* Jenny is in the process of becoming certified in midwifery. She was thrilled to get to see her first birth recently.

Her fascination with birthing is ironic. Molly's own birth was a complicated emergency; she was breech, upside down and backwards. The fetal monitor showed that she had been without oxygen for seven minutes. She was in ICU at Children's Hospital for a week. Kay and Jerry were told to expect possible cerebral palsy, retardation, blindness, deafness ... they prayed fervently. Today, Molly is healthy. Kay calls her their "miracle baby."

How did five girls gain the knowledge to succeed in so many endeavors? Did they do it alone? Not in this family! Mom and Dad and the five girls are one unit; they help each other, they care deeply about each other; they cheer each other in victories and cry together in disappointments; music, love and faith are the ties that bind them.

Kay says, "We firmly believe that every child should learn at least some music basics. Since the girls were tiny, music has filled our home. Jerry plays classical guitar. I play viola. The girls play everything else!"

Asked whether she ever hit the wall homeschooling five girls, Kay responded, "There was one time when 2 ½ year-old Jenny came to me with big, wide eyes and said, 'Mommy, will you teach me?' My teacher's heart began to flutter. Then it sank. Jenny wanted to learn how to fly!"

These extraordinary parents see their state and nation as a mission field. They actively support right-thinking, qualified candidates for public office who promote policies that benefit families. Kay and Jerry feel a heavy responsibility to involve the children in that effort, saying, "If our children need to be taught, we feel responsible to provide the teaching; if the nation is crumbling, we feel responsible to be part of the solution. Our kids were quite young when we first waved signs together on the corner for good conservative candidates."

And what do the girls have to say about the state of the nation?

Molly: "Dear America: We do not *deserve* anything. We, the people have, by the grace of God, been granted the freedom to *obtain* things through our own hard work. That is what originally made ours a secure and prosperous nation."

Jenny: "Instead of compromising our values in order to 'get along' I hope we can unify under our founding principles and make the fundamental changes needed to turn our nation around."

Katie Jo: "For 2016 and beyond, my hope is for a return to the values upon which our great nation was founded: faith in the Almighty, respect for individual liberty and limited government power."

Kay had the opportunity to go, expenses paid, to the International Conference on Climate Change, presented by the Heartland Institute in New York City. She says, "It was overwhelming the amount of critical information shared in the excellent presentations. So few people understand how this power-grab hoax called *Climate Change* will devastate the poor of our world. Their aim is to hobble first world economies!" Kay went to work and presented the facts of "Climate Change" to ad hoc and organized community groups, including at the Leadership Institute in Washington, DC, while daughter, Jill, interned there. Kay has also had about a dozen letters on a variety of other subjects published in the Wall Street Journal.

Jill writes this about her mom:

"My mom fostered a spirit of openness and honesty in our conversations, and always took time to just sit and talk with us, without an agenda. But those conversations turned out to be educational, and were a version of what Scripture tells us to do; teach our children as we sit at home and as we walk along the road, so instead of growing up with only my own immature thoughts to lead me, I grew up with years of wisdom leading me through those conversations.

"Now, at age 26, I count her as one of my closest friends. We can talk on the phone for hours on end, about everything under the sun. We laugh together a lot, she gives me advice, and she allows me to give her advice.

"It was fun growing up as a Buccola girl! The quiet mornings at our separate desks working on math, science, and history; the louder middays taking turns practicing various musical instruments; the overly talkative meal times, the eighteen 'forts' we built in the woods behind our first house; arguing over who got to get Jenny and Molly up from their naps when they were babies; eating junk food when mom was out of town and Daddy was in charge of nutritional choices; our traditional slumber party the night before Christmas in which Katie Jo makes us all tell her what boys we have crushes on, but she won't share what boy she likes; Mami (German for Mommy) reading *The Story of Liberty* out loud to us while as many of us as possible pile on her lap; the innumerable band concerts, harp and piano recitals, and *Daughters of Zion* practice session; eating boiled eggs for breakfast on the way to debate tournaments; the tears shed each time we boarded planes for college; the amazing experience of standing up in a sister's wedding, etc.

"It's so much fun to be a Buccola girl now! We have so much in common, it is great fun to spend time together."

Molly gives us this glimpse into how important her Dad is in her life:

"I went to a wedding in 2012 and this considerate single mother who worked with my Dad remarked that our Dad was such an amazing, loving and patient dude. She said she saw it in the confidence we girls had that her own daughter didn't get. She said she tried everything in her power to tell her daughter how beautiful she was, how talented she was, but it just wasn't the same as hearing it from a father. She said we Buccola girls will marry good, strong, enduring, loving husbands 'because you know what to look for.' She said that we will see when we are older what our Dad means to us, how *he made us who we are, just by being who he is.*'

"From gently rocking a kicking, fussing baby girl, to driving us home from our first fender-bender, his steadfast love for us is always there. No matter what disrespect this youngster shows to her Dad's wishes, his response is always mercy. His never-wavering mercy to me, his daughter, no matter my thoughtlessness or selfish acts, gives me a vivid picture of **our merciful Father in Heaven** *who made us who we are, just by being I AM.*"

This accomplished family is an example of a traditional family in America that prays together, works together, supports each other and loves each other. Kay and Jerry Buccola's dream of family has come true because everybody works at it - together. They wouldn't have it any other way.

> *"You shall therefore, lay up these words of mine in your heart and in your soul, and you shall bind them as a sign upon your hand, and they shall be as frontlets between your eyes. And you shall teach them to your children, talking of them when you are sitting in your house, and when you are walking by the way, and when you lie down, and when you rise."* Deut 11.18,19 RSV

What principles and values from this story are also foundational in your life?

From Kay and Jerry _____

_____

From the girls _____

_____

TIM MCMAHON AND CYNTHIA MONTAGNE

Photo: Joel Sorrell

WHAT WILL YOUR LEGACY BE?

AN ENTREPRENEURIAL LEGACY

"We are possibility people! We don't close the door. We're not afraid of risks!"
Tim McMahon & Cynthia Montagne

Tim McMahon, a fourth generation Seattleite, was raised on a farm in Woodinville, Washington with four siblings, was educated at Christ the King in North Seattle, at the Irish Christian Brothers Boarding School in Vancouver, Canada and graduated from Ingraham High School in 1965.

As Tim was working his way through college, his draft number was about to come up, so he enlisted and completed six years active duty in the Marine Corps Reserves during which he finished his education, graduating from the University of Washington in 1971.

The economy was terrible in Seattle. There were few opportunities for a job. An avid skier, Tim saw an ad for a ski shop manager in Montana and left Seattle for what he thought would be a year or so. Fifteen years later, Tim, whose degree is in Literature, had become an engineer. Management at Discovery Basin Ski Lodge at Georgetown Lake, Montana was sorely lacking. Tim stepped in and in two years, developed it from a one chair ski resort to a first class operation.

He opened his first ski shop, then another in Missoula, another in Hamilton and took over the ski rental shop at Discovery. He sold bikes in the summer and skis in the winter.

Then there were three years of no snow, the unions went on strike and Tim watched as the last smelter in Anaconda folded. So did his ski shops. Looking for the next challenge, Tim got a job at Big Sky Resort, Montana, where he successfully developed and sold their vacation properties.

"I hired this pretty little whitewater sports photographer named Cynthia to film the story of Big Sky and got to know her. I knew she was the one for me."

Cynthia adds, "Tim was a few years older than me but he was the most humble, surprising person I'd ever met. And he was a racer! He has an amazing skiing talent, so I thought, 'Okay, he's cool, he passes' and we dated." They married in Bozeman in 1984.

Seeking a better economy in which to thrive, the couple moved back to Seattle and Tim became a broker with First Western Properties, then opened his own firm, Washington Commercial Real Estate Services in 1990. Tim and Cynthia bought their first building and acquired and developed properties from Olympia to Everett in Washington State. The sports photographer with a degree in Speech and Hearing (Audiology) became a force to be reckoned with as a manager of commercial properties, self-taught.

Tim calls Cynthia his "rock" during those years, always encouraging him to go ahead and try and see what happens. Tim says, "Every morning, Cynthia would make sure my suit was pressed, that I had on a clean shirt and an okay tie and nudge me out the door, saying, 'Keep going. You can do it!'"

"People thought we had a big staff." Cynthia says. "It was just the two of us at first! I had a little desk in the corner of our bedroom and I just learned the business! With hard work and tenacity, our business grew and prospered."

In 1995, a group of business people in Lynnwood opened Prime Pacific Bank and asked Tim to serve as a Trustee. Years later, as

Chairman of the Board, Tim had the solemn responsibility of keeping the bank true to its fiduciary responsibilities to its shareholders.

Tim worked through the regulatory minefield and successfully sold the bank in the fall of 2016. He offers this frank assessment of what happened in the national financial community:

"There were some insider things going on that favored the larger banks and that got out of control, ending up punishing everybody. Bankers were told to reign in commercial real estate calling it a risk. The money supply dried up for developers.

"The other thing that happened, especially in Washington State, was that government regulations became so burdensome that business development from concept to shovel became a very, very difficult process. I don't understand how regulators got that powerful."

Tim and Cynthia survived that economic mess because of careful, expert planning, consistent hard work, faith and an indomitable "can do" spirit. That same spirit dwells within their two sons, of whom they are unabashedly proud.

Both of the boys are champion skiers and fly fishermen. Son Brandon earned a degree in Finance and Real Estate from the University of Denver. Second son, Connor, has a rare degree from Central Washington University in Global Wine Studies, which is the study, not of winemaking, but of the "business" of wine.

In 2010, Tim experienced something of a full circle back to his youth when he and Cynthia designed and built a home on the same site his dad owned back in the 1960's when Tim was a boy. It was a rustic cabin then, a getaway. Today the home is a welcoming masterpiece of design on 200 feet of Kitsap County waterfront.

The McMahon family skis together, fishes together, prays together and continues to be involved in their community.

In 2011, Cynthia organized the Shoreline Property Owners. The dozens of families living on the water were notified by postcard from the County that their property rights were being reduced. In response, she drafted a letter, hand-delivered it to each resident and held a meeting in their home. More than 30 people showed up. The county commissioner came and listened to the well-researched and heartfelt testimonies of residents who love the land and are stewards of it and some of the proposed changes were reversed! Give Cynthia Montagne a problem, she'll fix it.

In 2014, these two entrepreneurs decided it would be fun to learn to sail. So, they purchased a sailboat. Neither had sailed before, but so what? They could learn. The first extended trip to Desolation Sound was a three-week voyage and Tim says, "We had a blast and enjoyed every minute of it!" In 2017 they bought a Beneteau Oceanis 48-foot sailboat for a three and a half month long journey up the inside passage to Alaska. The trip will take them over 1500 miles on their boat with many risks and memorable experiences. They depart in May of 2017.

So, why does a 70-year old go sailing on an unknown adventure like this? According to Tim; "It has to do with life and not letting the moments slip by. Cynthia is a confident person and says 'we can do it,' so we do it. We don't want retirement to look like retirement, but rather an exploration of new journeys and learning new skills."

2016 was a landmark year for Tim and Cynthia as both of their sons married the perfect daughters-in-law in unforgettable ceremonies filled with tears of joy and followed by the newly blended families becoming one loving family unit.

Tim offers this advice to fathers: "If you think that once your children are grown that they no longer need you, you are sadly mistaken. We find that now that our children are adults, they need us more than ever as they are making life decisions, seeking advice and getting support through their struggles and disappointments. The boys need a father more than ever. A father's task is never finished. They will always need you to share ideas, listen to problems and applaud their successes."

Ever mindful of the needs of their church and community, the McMahon's philanthropy extends not only to organizations that are preserving our freedom, but also to the needy. They purchased a four-bedroom home for disadvantaged women with children. Then they joined hands with the Mission House, helping men overcome addiction. The director there, Mat Perkins, has had national requests to replicate such a program for women. With Tim and Cynthia's assistance, the Mission House is ready to open its first recovery house for women.

"We are very excited about this program," Tim says. "It is self-sustaining and has a proven system that turns lives around through hard work and principles taught in the Bible. We are hoping that in a short time Mission House will need an additional facility to accommodate demand and we will be there to help them and the local community secure that home.

"When Cynthia and I are gone, we don't want to be remembered as 'those nice people.' We want to leave a legacy that makes one scratch their heads and wonder 'what were they doing?' We will all be forgotten with time, so trying to create a remembrance seems futile. We want to pass on values to our children and to their children and support their families with education and visions. And we want to help our community. We don't measure success by money. We'd rather be remembered for the vision and life course that we leave for others to follow."

> *"Some say risk nothing, try only for the sure thing,*
> *Others say nothing gambled nothing gained,*
> *Go all out for your dream.*
> *Life can be lived either way, but for me,*
> *I'd rather try and fail, than never try at all, you see.*
> William F. O'Brien

What values and principles from this story are also foundational in your life?

From Tim _____

_____

From Cynthia _____

_____

SGT. JOHN HARSH, HOME FROM IRAQ

Photo: FrontSight Military Outreach

HELPING DISABLED
VETERANS

J ohn Michael Harsh, age 30, was born in Ashland, Oregon. He served five years as an infantry sergeant in the United States Marine Corps, including three combat tours in Iraq. John was a member of 3rd Battalion, 1st Division, Kilo Company, Weapon's Platoon in Fallujah. His was the first company of the first unit into the city. His unit was described as the "tip of the spear." His company was the point of that tip, meaning first line against the enemy.

Fallujah was one of the first major assaults of the Iraq War. Americans were anxiously watching and listening to the media for any news of the battle. John's mother, Lynn, knew when the assault was imminent and was constantly on alert for any word of her son.

She heard nothing. *For three weeks.*

By the end of the third week, friends and family worried about Lynn's health, thinking she may have to go to the hospital. Worry and fear for her son dominated her daily activities. Then came the word that her son had survived the critical assault into Fallujah. And, indeed, his mother was hospitalized for a time to regain her strength and well-being. John recovered from the assault and readied for a second and last tour after which he was sent home.

The joy of his homecoming was muted when friends and family witnessed that John was struggling to adjust to being back home. He had seen some of his fellow soldiers killed in action and experienced too many close and ear-splitting explosions in Iraq.

His mother, Lynn recalls that her son's early Christian training was still in there, but that when he got home, John had lost some of his natural intuition to know right from wrong, and his normally very good judgment had been seriously damaged by the scourge of war. John was suffering from the unseen, often misunderstood illness called PTSD.

Post-Traumatic Stress Disorder is variously defined as a debilitating psychological condition triggered by a major traumatic event, such as rape, war, a terrorist act, death of a loved one, a natural disaster, or a catastrophic accident. It is marked by upsetting memories or thoughts of the ordeal, "blunting" of emotions and sometimes severe personality changes. Before 1980, PTSD was known as shell shock or battle fatigue because of its more common manifestation in war veterans.

John says, "When I came home from the last tour in Iraq, I felt like I was giving the people at church PTSD by telling them how I got PTSD; they couldn't relate. I don't blame them. The only people I knew who could relate weren't following Christ. I felt like I didn't belong anywhere.

"I had met Danielle while I was still in the Marines. She didn't want anything to do with me. I lived in Oregon and had recently recommitted my life to Christ. Danielle was single and living in California. We reconnected through a mutual friend. Our first real date was our wedding in Las Vegas."

John continued to struggle until a friend told him about FrontSight Military Outreach, an organization with a stated mission of helping disabled veterans turn their injuries into assets. John walked into FrontSight and, he says, for the first time since he got home, he felt comfortable. He was surrounded by men who knew what he was talking about. They were familiar with the thoughts he expressed because they had been through it and come out the other side to help men like John.

He stuck close to the guys at FrontSight and, in that welcome camaraderie, could feel the dread, the anger, the confusion and myriad other feelings peel away. He knew that he could pay it forward to other vets in need.

So, he opened a gym in the back of the warehouse at FrontSight. They named it FrontSight Fitness. It was so successful that at the end of the first year, the FrontSight board asked John to become the Commanding Officer of the entire outreach. He had found a community of Christian veterans he never thought he would find and his life changed dramatically.

FrontSight has operations in San Bernardino, Riverside, North Orange and East Los Angeles counties. Their aim is to build a replicable model that can be operated elsewhere to serve at least 10,000 veterans within five years. John says, "They're out there. We know it. And we're here to help them. FrontSight probably saved my life."

The organization works with hundreds of veterans ranging from the Korean War veterans to 19-year old recruits. Their mission is to address the whole person, to make recovery available for body, mind and spirit. They reject a victim mentality. Owning up to their individual circumstances and moving forward is the plan as they live meaningful lives defined by what they have gained, not by what they've lost.

The veterans are treated as worthy stewards of their future, not unfortunate victims of the past. FrontSight works on the core reasons for veteran suicide and dependence; the causes of the grim statistic that fifteen times as many veterans have died from suicide as have died from direct combat injuries in the last two wars.

John says, "At FrontSight, we seek the Kingdom first. Our unwavering commitment is to support veterans in spiritual, emotional and physical recovery so they can find meaningful work for their families and their community. In doing so, the Lord has brought many supporters through our doors. Some are vets, some are investors, some are volunteers. Others are family members, and politicians. We don't receive any direct support from the government, but our pursuit of God's will has won us favor in the eyes of man; namely the Veteran's Administration. Our reputation has positioned us as one of their top referrals and we work closely with the VA to ensure the best care for our vets."

Friends notice the difference FrontSight is making in John's progress. "Every aspect of my life is better," John explains, "but best of all, my son gets to grow up with a well-balanced and Christ-fearing father."

John began to see his marriage to Danielle and his love for his son, Kaelum, now two and a half years old, with a new realization of the tremendous responsibility he has as a husband and a father.

John, Danielle and Kaelum Harsh

On June 26, 2016, a ceremony was held, arranged and lovingly produced by Danielle's parents and John's mother, Lynn, at which John and Danielle renewed their marriage vows. It was held at the Christmas House in Rancho Cucamonga. The officiant was a man named Pastor Rudy, who was in Special Forces in the Marine Corps and later founded a ministry called SERT which rescues women from sex trafficking worldwide. John's best man was his best friend. He says, "The Lord continues to connect people when we align our lives with His will. I am deeply grateful for His mercies to me."

The attendees for the ceremony were John's family members and many men from FrontSight filled the rest of the seats. They have each other's back.

John's mother travels a lot in her work. He remembers one day after about a year back home, he drove his mother to the airport. "I dropped my mom off," John says, "and I felt a very foreign emotion; I missed her, and I couldn't remember the last time I felt that. For me, PTSD is the distance between where I live and reality. I feel that distance closing now. Praise God."

> *"Therefore, since we are justified by faith, we have peace with God through our Lord Jesus Christ. Through him we have obtained access to this grace in which we stand and we rejoice in our hope of sharing the glory of God."*
>
> Rom 5.1,2 RSV

What principles and values from this story are also foundational in your life?

From John _____

_____

99

 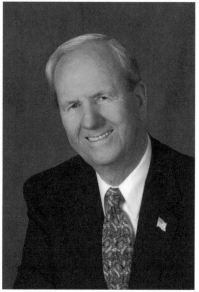

PAT MOLEN   GERALD R. MOLEN

Photos: Karen Weyer Photography

WHAT WILL YOUR LEGACY BE?

A LEGACY OF HUMILITY

P roducer Jerry Molen is a giant of the motion picture industry with a career that spans over 50 years. His prodigious record of achievement includes more than 20 iconic films including *Jurassic Park* and *Jurassic Park: The Lost World*, *Minority Report*, *Days of Thunder*, *"batteries not included,"* *Hook*, *Rain Man*, *Twister*, *Casper*, *The Flintstones*, the Academy Award-winning *Schindler's List* and many more.

Definitely not a member of the Hollywood elite, this gentle giant rose from humble beginnings to the pinnacle of success as one of the highest acclaimed producers in his industry. None of that notoriety and glitter has shaken his dedication to family, faith and freedom.

Montana is in his genes. He remembers fondly the days of his youth on the family farm in Fairfield and moving to Great Falls in 1943: "I am the eldest of four brothers. My parents were middle class. My dad had an entrepreneurial spirit and work ethic he passed on to us. My mom was a homemaker first. But she was a champion to her kids."

It was in 1946 that the family moved to Southern California seeking a new life. Jerry's dad found a piece of property across the street from Republic Pictures and built a small café that was the breadwinner for the family of nine; Jerry, his three brothers, three sisters and mom and dad. His mom worked the restaurant and as caterer to movie companies.

101

Jerry served three years in the Marine Corps, leaving with the rank of Sergeant. When he got home, his historic career in film had its genesis right there at the movie studio across the street. His first job was changing tires on the studio trucks and the rest is history.

Jerry confides, "I truly believe the faith and religious instruction I received from my parents is responsible for my personal behavior and in large part, my character. It was those traits that carried me through living and working within the Hollywood establishment and allowed me to stick with my morals and values. I have a deep reverence for my faith and am so grateful for the guidance it has given me."

During the filming of Schindler's List, the Academy Award-winning Best Picture of 1993, Jerry experienced an unseen guiding force that is to this day unexplained but it was real because he lived it. He tells the story:

"The early filming required snow on the ground and was to take place first in the schedule. When I arrived in Poland to prepare for the filming there was no snow on the ground. In fact, as the scheduled date of principal photography got closer, there was still no snow and we found ourselves looking for ways to mitigate the problem. It was a worry for everyone involved. Just one week prior to filming and the day that the film's Director, Steven Spielberg arrived, it began to snow! It continued for the next few days, allowing us to begin our filming schedule on time and with great effect.

"About three weeks into the schedule, we realized we were running out of scenes that required snow. We began making plans for eliminating the snow that would surely be visible and a detriment to our filming. We made plans to film an interior scene on that Saturday to give us cover while we figured out how to remove the snow.

"On Sunday morning I opened my drapes to see the snow had disappeared overnight. We were totally amazed! An abnormal weather front had come through the area and the temperature rose enough to allow the snow to melt overnight! This phenomenon was explained within our ranks as "a divine Hand" watching over our production.

"A couple of weeks later Mr. Spielberg informed me he wanted to add a particular scene that required snow and very cold weather. Not much chance of that happening so we began an effort to find snow-making machines or a way of hauling snow in from the mountains. But, once again, a storm came in and the weather turned very cold. It began to snow again! We took advantage of the situation, changed our schedule and filmed the desired footage. Upon completion of the required filming, the weather turned back and we resumed our original schedule.

"We lost no time, did not lose any necessary footage or required scenes. Yes, we were watched over by 'a Divine Hand.' Of that, there can be no doubt!"

At the peak of his fame, including 17 movies with Steven Spielberg, Jerry met Dinesh D'Souza, and says this about his great friend:

"I've had the honor of working with some of Hollywood's finest filmmakers: Spielberg, Pollack, Reidel, Ashby. My career was capped by working with Dinesh D'Souza. He is a great American, political activist, speaker, producer, director, husband, philanthropist, philosopher and renowned author.

"Imagine a young man of 17 arriving in America from India with nothing more than a dream. Yet he immediately recognized the promise of America. He knew what he had to do. He got an education and committed himself to excellence. His wife, Debbie, is a fantastic partner for him and honors him with her intelligence, beauty and dedication. I am proud to call them my friends."

In 2012, Jerry was catapulted into the conservative public eye in partnership with Dinesh to produce the blockbuster movie, *2016: Obama's America*, followed by the documentary, *AMERICA*, imagine the world without her."

On September 5th 2015, Jerry suffered a stroke. He had been heavily involved with the making and pre-marketing of the documentary, *"America,"* and candidly says that he completely wore himself out.

"My body was telling me to 'slow down and smell the roses.' My stay in the hospital was short with no heavy damage (thankfully) except for minimal memory loss. I have returned to full throttle -well, slowed down a bit -and continue to work, knowing that the good Lord watches over me, guides me and cares for me. Besides, I have a lot of work yet to do."

Projects after *"America"* included an important documentary entitled *"The Abolitionists."* It reveals the actual efforts of a dedicated group of men and women who are determined to rescue children from the travesty of child sex trafficking, a deplorable form of slavery that plagues more than 2 million children around the world. That was followed by helping Dinesh D'Souza produce a documentary based on his latest book, *Stealing America*. The film, entitled *Hillary's America*, gives a political oversight of the Democratic Party and how the Clintons have emerged.

Jerry says that one of the best blessings in his life has been to watch the success and fortitude of his brothers and sisters: "My brother Ken earned a Bachelor's Degree at Brigham Young University, a Master's Degree from Chapman College, graduated from Loyola Dental College of Chicago and earned his pre-doctoral candidacy in education from the University of Southern California.

"Dean also graduated with a BS from Brigham Young, served as Captain in the U.S. Air Force and received his DDS from the University of Washington. Bruce attended Brigham Young, served as Captain in the Air Force before earning his DDS at the University of California at Los Angeles and a degree in orthodontics from the University of Washington. They are all generous and highly successful people. Each of them worked their way through college. They had no financial help from outside sources. They did it themselves. I am very proud of them."

Jerry himself has received honorary doctorate degrees in Fine Arts from the University of Montana and in Performing and Visual Arts from Southern Utah University in addition to the undying gratitude of the many millions of moviegoers who enjoy his iconic films.

"Growing up," he says, "we never knew we were poor. Our parents blessed us by teaching us God, country, responsibility, discipline, positive attitudes and grateful hearts. They taught us the need for hard work. Each of us earned our way, ever mindful of the gifts from our Founding Fathers and the free enterprise system of government that gave us the freedom to succeed"

But if you know Jerry Molen, you know that he considers Pat, his lovely wife of 62 years, his biggest blessing. In his own words:

"Without a doubt, Pat and I have a relationship authorized by the good Lord in Heaven. As a young man I was blessed with finding her and falling in love with her. That feeling has never changed. It has only been enhanced by her believing in me, caring for me, loving me and cherishing the finite time we have on earth together. I am confident, encouraged and secure that after whatever amount of time we share here in our mortal lives, we will share the promise of eternity together.

"As the issues and moments of life and career have unfolded, I know that I could not have accomplished my goals without her. We have two wonderful children who have blessed us with four grandchildren and six great-grandchildren. Our eldest son is Steven and our precious daughter is Lorion. We are so very proud of both of them."

Jerry and Pat held an event where about 150 colleagues and friends flew in from all over the country to honor them on their 60th wedding anniversary. One wonders what conversation that weekend may have sparked the next project for one of America's greatest film producers.

"The reward for humility and fear of the Lord is riches and honor and life. Prov 22.4 RSV

What principles and values from this story are also foundational in your life?

From Jerry _____

_____

From Pat _____

_____

105

ZORKA FOWLER AS A YOUNG WOMAN

SURVIVING ON THE
IRON RANGE

Zorka was born in 1931 to her widowed mother, Mary, who was pregnant most of the nine years of her marriage to Nichola. Nichola died three months before Zorka was born. She was her mother's sixth child.

Nichola worked in the mines of The Iron Range in Hibbing, Minnesota where it was hot and humid in the summer and could go to 55 degrees below zero in the winter. The Range was a series of pits covering one hundred miles, a longer stretch than the Panama Canal. From these mines came the iron for the steel that built America.

The hardest work in the open pit mines was given to the tens of thousands of immigrants, like Nichola, who dug the ore. The mining families lived in daily deprivation, in a community of shack-like houses, owned by the company. Families paid one dollar a month for their meager housing and received barely enough money to put food on the table. Pensions were promised. Promises were broken.

Zorka reflects on how hard it must have been for her mother, who never complained. Six children. No husband. No money. Little food. No hope. That was NOT the fulfillment of the Great American Dream to which her mother had traveled ten years before from the Carpathian Mountain Valley (known today as East Poland.) The family now faced a bleak and uncertain future in one of hundreds of little houses on a road along The Iron Range in a section named "Pool Location." (*Each mining community section was identified as a "Location."*)

Zorka and her brother and sisters were assigned chores as soon as they could walk. They kept the house clean. Mama planted the garden, made bread and did the cooking. The children picked berries, competing with an occasional black bear, weeded the garden and carried water in a pail from the neighborhood pump. They milked the cow and led it to pasture. Their clothes came from the County charity collections in and around Hibbing.

Of her winter coat, Zorka recalls, "It was a spring coat without lining and was torn in places. Mama repaired it. The coat was a terrible aqua color but with other layers under it, I kept warm in the bitter cold. The saying of the time, 'Use it up, wear it out, 'make it do or do without' surely applied to us."

There was joy to be found in this barren place of sweat and tears, even in the family's challenging circumstances. When Zorka talks about her life in the "Pool", she smiles as she eloquently recalls the happy times of her childhood.

"We children loved being with each other and our friends. We explored the fields around us. In the summer, we would lie on our backs and look at the sky, listening to the sounds of insects humming, buzzing. At times, it became a cacophonous but melodious mix of buzzes, hums, whizzes and chirps. We loved the smell of the sweet and spicy grass, weeds, wild flowers and damp soil. The warm sunshine and cool earth provided a feeling that there was a world beyond The Iron Range. There *was* hope."

There was a community store to visit and the Big Rock on which the children could stand and see the fairgrounds. The Rock was only about four feet high but could accommodate a half dozen or more kids. It was the gathering place for Zorka and her sister Anne to meet up with wonderful friends like Fanny and Dolly, who lived down the road.

"The Rock was always there, waiting for us," says Zorka. If we got enough money, we'd go to the community store and buy a box of marshmallows, cut sticks from the trees, make a small fire and roast them. We felt we were truly in Paradise."

Zorka and her friends

The school bus came down the road to pick up the children in each house when the weather allowed. If there was ice and snow, no bus came. They had to get to school, so the children dressed in layers of clothing and walked the dirt road four blocks to a bus stop. There, they waited for the bus to take them to school. In particularly cold and snowy weather, they linked themselves together with a long rope so no one got lost on the long, winding road.

Zorka, her siblings and their mother survived 16 years in Pool Location, until one day, a directive from the Company was received by all residents, stating that it was time to move out. The family moved their meager belongings to what Zorka called "a real house on a real street."

"Alas," Zorka confides, "when I went back, later in life, The Rock, which was always there, the store which was always there, the houses, the roads – all were gone, swallowed up over the decades by the pit. I stood on the rampart that used to be those precious, life-giving places of my girlhood; that had this miraculous way of erasing the sad days with their natural beauty that was such a contrast to the dirty, back-breaking work in the mines. Those precious places that always beckoned us to come and come again were no more. I could only *imagine* where they had been. But my memories I will cherish all of my life."

Listening to this beautiful, successful lady's story today, it is hard to imagine that she had such a childhood. She speaks with great joy in her heart about her youth, choosing to remember all that was good. She worked hard, studied hard, graduated high school and later earned a Master's Degree in Special Education from the University of San Francisco. Zorka became a teacher and a principal, a model, an actress and a licensed pilot.

She married the love of her life, Kirk Fowler, another child of the Great Depression, who was an electrical engineer. He founded a successful heavy equipment company and also served as a Scoutmaster. Kirk was a voracious reader who started studying the Bible at age 15 and lived his life by Micah, chapter six: *"What is expected of thee, oh man but to do justly, to love mercy and to walk humbly before God."* Kirk passed away three years ago. Zorka still mourns her loss, but enjoys her two grown daughters, Shannon and Shawn, seven grandchildren and two great grandchildren.

Education is her passion. She says, "I support very good, proven programs for our children and our teachers. I worry about what is happening in education in our great country."

Zorka gives all credit for her success in life to her mother, Mary, saying "Mama died at age 95. She raised us with abiding love through terrible hardships, back-breaking work, perseverance and a lot of prayer. She was very proud of all of us. Did she participate in the Great American Dream? I would say, yes! Mama was one of the achievers who left the closed cultures of Europe for the free society of America. At the very core of these immigrants was something indestructible that consisted of faith, a conscience that knew instinctively the right thing to do, and a heart that was willing and eager to do it.

"Now, in America, it is not so easy to build such character without hardship. God grant that in our easier life today, we can still build character, understand the blessings of hard work and the foundations of a moral society. God grant that as the 21ˢᵗ Century continues, we can stop the erosion of cultural and moral principles which the people of the 20ᵗʰ Century worked so hard to protect and who helped to make America the greatest nation on God's green earth."

> *"Fear not, for I am with you; be not dismayed for I am your God; I will strengthen you, I will help you, I will uphold you with my righteous right hand."*
>
> Is 41.10 RSV

What principles and values from this story are also foundational in your life?

From Zorka _____

_____

From Mary _____

_____

DIANE AND LARRY SUNDQUIST

WHAT WILL YOUR LEGACY BE?

A LEGACY OF OBEDIENCE

"**S**undquist Homes is God's business, not mine." That's how Larry Sundquist sees his work life and his personal life.

He says, "I have a line from God's Word on the wall at home. It says *'If you have faith, nothing shall be impossible for you.'* That daily reminder has helped me get through some tough days as a builder."

In 1974, Larry founded Sundquist Homes, *A Family of Companies* which is highly regarded throughout the Pacific Northwest as a premier builder of quality homes. In 1977, he became involved with Seattle Master Builders Association, becoming chairman of the Snohomish County Counsel, followed by a board position in the Association. He eventually became president in 1988.

Concurrent with leading the SMBA, Larry became very involved in the Building Industry Association of Washington and was their legislative chairman for a number of years. He received the Chairman's award from the Association of Washington Business. A longtime Rotarian, in 1995, Larry was further honored with the Rotary Foundation Paul Harris Fellowship Award.

Larry has turned the day to day leadership of his company over to others. He says, "Actually, in the mid-1990's I began to dissolve responsibilities with the building industry and other business activities to devote more of my time to church and other Kingdom pursuits."

Larry accepted Christ at a Lutheran church winter youth camp. His wife and partner in ministry, Diane, accepted Christ in a Pentecostal church as a teenager. Larry reflects on that time of his life:

"Like so many other young people, we drifted away from the Lord in our early years and it was after we married and were having kids in our early 30's that brought us back to the church. Even after attending church it was not until the kids were getting a little bit older and I was contemplating what I was going to do when I grew up, that a radical change happened in my life.

"In October of 1997, I was invited by our Pastor to join a group of four to investigate the possibility of doing a mission's project in South India and to speak at a Pastor's conference. I reluctantly went on this trip and it truly challenged my comfort level.

"After being there a few days I was glad to be leaving this God-forsaken land and happy to be headed back to the States. However, upon my return and sharing the experience with family and friends I quickly grew a new desire to return. Over the next year, a lot of planning took place and an India team was formed at Westgate Chapel, my church.

"In 1998, the Malabar Missions project was launched with the placement of 78 pastors at different parts of the Malabar region in the northern part of the state of Kerala. In November of that year I was part of a team to return to minister and be with these pastors for a pastor's conference. Over the next few years I led the India team and returned to India a couple more times.

"In 2001, I was denied a visa to enter India for unknown reasons. By this time, I had made friends with many people in different parts of India. When I notified some of them about the odd denial of my visa privilege, one friend, a pastor in Bombay, started having his congregation pray for me and a businessman from there invited me to come on a Business Visa which I applied for and received! Upon returning from that trip, I applied for a ten-year business visa and for permission to open a business in India. Both of these were granted and I made a couple more trips to India."

Larry remembers one of the more harrowing trips to India:

"In February of 2006, Diane and I were in for a shock. We traveled to India for the purpose of speaking at a Bible College graduation and attending to other ministry activities. Upon arrival, the immigration officer started scouring his computer and my passport and we were ushered into an office where we began to be interrogated.

"The officers there were very friendly and eventually, after seeing all my paperwork, really wanted to help but as the night wore on and the British airline flight that I had to be returned on was sitting on the ground waiting for people who wanted to go, the authorities finally produced a paper that showed that I was banned from India for life. So off I went to the British airline flight and returned to London. Diane stayed behind with friends and gave my speech at the Bible College. She spent two weeks doing all the activities we had intended to do together. Diane was beyond her comfort level doing this."

Diane giving Larry's speech; beside her,
Dr. Idicheria Ninan, seminary president.

For nine years, Larry attempted to appeal to the government and different groups, trying to get a visa to return. In mid-2015, he was granted a six-month tourist visa and in late August 2015, returned to India.

"The flight arrived in the middle of the night. I was more than apprehensive and worried about getting in since I did not really know how I got this visa. In Seattle, many people were praying for me.

"As I walked to the immigration desk I was praying about which officer I should walk up to. I eventually selected a young lady who was very friendly at first but as she searched through the computer and looked at my passport, I shuddered, remembering my experience almost ten years earlier. A supervisor was called to the desk and many questions were asked. They spoke together in their local language and finally told me to go ahead. Once I reached the clearing area where I was to go through metal detectors and put my bags on the scanner, the supervisor who questioned me earlier came up, pulled me out of the line and began asking me more questions. He eventually waived me through.

"I approached the metal detectors and a uniformed immigration officer walked up to me and said, 'Are you a pastor?' I responded 'no, I am a home builder' and headed through the metal detector. Little did I know, that man was actually sent to help usher me through any more problems.

"When I got to the customs area, I was standing, waiting for my suitcase and a uniformed customs officer was walking toward me. At this point, I was dripping with sweat and nervous from the whole ordeal. I felt great relief when he walked up to me, shook my hand and said 'Praise the Lord!' I knew God had intervened."

This trip was not about ministering. It was about visiting and encouraging dear friends and seeing what had been happening in India over the last ten years since Larry and Diane had been there. While there, Larry was honored and blessed by people and organizations that they had been supporting all those years. The trip was a never-to-be-forgotten time of encouragement and blessing to both of them.

In 2003, Larry and Diane made a decision to start a family foundation. They named it the Natan Foundation. Natan is derived from the Hebrew verb meaning "to give." The meaning of the name in Jewish culture could be rendered He or God has given or He will give.

Larry says, "We started the foundation for several reasons. The two primary reasons were we wanted to be able to give more anonymously and secondly, to be able to save money in a separate entity where we could distribute it as we were led to do and not be forced to give money because we wanted a tax deduction in a certain year.

"Over the last twelve years, Natan has given money to numerous charitable causes both here in the United States and abroad. Our primary goals abroad have been for evangelism and in America, to influence national public policy. Prior to the 2007-2008 recession, when the Foundation was providing a lot of funding, we did have a part-time person working for us. Since that time we have a bookkeeper managing the affairs of the Foundation and helping implement decisions on funding that come from us, but at times our kids are also involved in some of that decision making.

"My role in missions has mostly been in leadership and oversight. I have not directly led anyone to the Lord, although I have certainly ministered to people. Our foreign work has involved some brick and mortar projects. We have supported a number of pastors who do evangelistic work. We have supported a nursery school and schools for impoverished kids. At one point we were feeding nearly 150 kids every day.

"Today, Natan supports nursery schools, sewing schools and is just starting a class to teach women in rural areas how to use computers. Larry traveled to Hungary and Romania where his church is associated with a ministry to the Gypsies. In Romania, the conditions in the camps were horrible. Living in utter despair, they were the saddest people I have ever seen - far worse than anything I ever saw in India. A family of six was living in a hut with a thatched roof that was leaking snow. We made some modest financial commitments to activities to enable them to support their families.

"We do this work because we love the Lord and we want to see as many people as possible come to know Him. Today I believe the United States is as big a mission field as some of the areas we have worked in India. This is why we have supported so many activities here in the United States dealing with public policy and prayer. The United States simply needs Jesus and revival."

Larry's activities have not been exclusively global missions. In 2000, Larry took leadership of a project to complete a church in Seattle's Rainier Valley. The church had sat dormant for over 15 years. Larry rallied volunteers, gathered donations from subcontractors and suppliers and the church was completed.

"I have been directly responsible for starting one ministry which is the Family Policy Institute of Washington. The genesis of this came as I was sitting on our patio at our place in Lake Chelan, talking with Tony Perkins from Family Research Council about Christian engagement in public policy. Over the last ten years, the Family Policy Institute of Washington has flourished and grown to a very active organization with thousands of supporters and six employees. I continue to serve as board chairman.

"During that time period I became the only non-pastor board member of a group that we started, called Mayday for Marriage, which stood for traditional marriage between one man and one woman.

"This group conducted a large rally at Safeco Field in Seattle in 2004 and later that year, a national rally on the Washington D.C. Mall. It was attended by an estimated 200,000 people. After a couple years of existence this organization was completely turned over to the late and beloved Pastor Ken Hutcherson.

"In 2005, because of all the efforts to save traditional marriage, my pastor was led to start an organization called *Sound the Alarm*. Later, this organization changed its name to *Church Awakening* and its primary purpose now is to encourage pastors in prayer and revival. I encouraged our pastor in this endeavor, supported it financially and was one of the founding board members. I would not want to take credit for starting it.

"I believe very strongly in foreign missions even in today's dangerous world. I believe everyone should go on a mission trip at least once in their life. I believe God can really speak to us when we are out in a foreign place ministering to people. Even in a world that seems very unsafe today, I believe there are many places we can go and be relatively safe as Americans.

"Prayer is a vital part of going and being on a mission trip. I have felt hugely impacted by the prayers of people at home when I have been on these trips.

"There has probably been no greater need for prayer than when I returned to India in August of 2015. It was probably 85 degrees, 95% humidity and I was nervous and sweating, but I was still able to approach that experience with confidence that God would get me through because of the prayers I knew were happening and that I could give God the glory for it afterward.

"Our kids have all helped out with *Family Policy Institute of Washington* over the years. There is really no balance in my life. It's one big exciting roller coaster ride with work, ministry, and three awesome grandchildren! Diane and I have an attitude we will just go with God in whatever we do."

> *"If you have faith .... nothing shall be impossible for you."*
> Mt 21.21 RSV

What principles and values from this story are also foundational in your life?

From Larry _____

_____

From Diane _____

_____

BRENT JONES, FAMED NFL TIGHT END,
SAN FRANCISCO 49ERS

A MARRIAGE MADE IN HEAVEN

B rent Jones retired from the National Football League in 1999 with an impressive on the field record as one of the game's top Tight Ends:

- Regular Season: 143 games / 417 REC / 5195 YDS / 12.5 AVG / 33 TDs
- Post Season: 19 games / 60 REC / 740 YDS / 5 TDs
- 12 seasons, 11 with the San Francisco 49ers, 1 with the Pittsburgh Steelers...earning All-Pro honors, 4 appearances at the Pro Bowl, 3 Super Bowl Championship titles.

But there is much more to the man than being a great NFL player. Brent was very involved with the 49er team Bible study and was called upon numerous times to represent the team at functions. His off the field awards confirm not *what* he is, but *who* he is:

- 1996 - True Value Man of the Year, San Francisco 49ers
- 1997 - CityTeam Ministries Good Samaritan Award
- 1998 - Bart Starr Award recipient – given annually to the NFL player who best exemplifies outstanding character and leadership in the home, on the field and in the community.

Awarded to the winner each year by Bart Starr at the Athlete in Action-hosted Super Bowl Breakfast, sanctioned by the NFL in the Super Bowl City.

- 30-year commitment to San Jose/Silicon Valley YoungLife with the Brent Jones Open tournament held each year in May at Almaden Country Club, which raises funds and awareness for kids to experience a Christian Summer Camp like no other.

After 30 years of marriage, Brent's wife, Dana is happy to tell you she is still unabashedly in love:

"What a privilege to discuss one of my favorite topics, my husband and best friend, love of my life – Brent Michael Jones. I met Brent when I was 19 and honestly fell in love and was so intrigued by him from day one. I loved his smile and he was so focused and funny. I always knew what he was thinking. He would talk to me about everything like he didn't want to miss a chance to share with me. This has never changed. We are in constant contact no matter where we are in the world.

"Some situations we have had to endure in pro football have been difficult, but our relationship is strong enough that things have always been easy with Brent. Truly. We both know that there are reasons for everything and we don't second guess why. We have always wondered how God is going to use us on all of the paths He has placed us.

"Brent is such a well-grounded and stable man. Spending life together has been my daily pleasure, truly! No, I don't wander around wearing rose-colored glasses, and yes we discuss and disagree with each other, but we have a faith foundation which has, from the very beginning, bonded us into this great team. Brent makes me better, encourages me to be better and has seen potential in me at times of shaken confidence. He has been the wind beneath my wings. Reciprocally, I am certain Brent feels the same.

"We have always had such a deep trust in each other that no matter where we are, I represent us and he represents us and nothing will ever come between us. We don't nauseatingly talk about each other in the other's absence but it is known that we live out Song of Solomon 3:4: "I have found the one that my heart desires."

Brent and Dana's parents have played a huge role in the outcome of their children's lives. They became fast friends from the first meeting after a Santa Clara football game at Round Table Pizza. Brent's dad, Mike, was star quarterback at San Jose State in college, was drafted by the Oakland Raiders, but after an injury, he was given bus fare home to San Jose. He went on to be a much-loved high school teacher with a successful coaching career. Barbara loved teaching, but left the classroom to raise Brent and his brother Craig while making their home a showplace with her great sense of design.

Dana's parents provided all three of their girls with a strong foundation in the Christian faith and a strong love of sports. Dana's mom, Judy, extremely artistic and domestically talented, also attended, then felt led to teach Bible Study Fellowship classes for years. Her dad, Bob, was Chairman of their home church, very involved in the men's ministries including the men's BSF study. Bob was a Fisheries and Wildlife Biologist who taught Dana and her sisters all about the great outdoors. He was a very patient man. Bob passed away two years ago and is greatly missed. Dana enjoys attending Precepts Bible Studies and other Christian education seminars and conferences.

Dana says, "Both Brent's and my parents have been incredibly supportive and loving and so very funny. We have often said they should star in a reality TV show. Our family celebrations are precious memories, full of the fun and the love we all share."

The first ever NFL Prayer Circle, December 3, 1990

The Prayer Circle

In 1990, Brent was a central figure in planning and executing the *first ever* Prayer Circle of players on the field after an NFL game.

Twenty six years ago, on December 3, 1990, a crucial game was to be played between two 10-1 teams, each vying for another Super Bowl slot. The New York Giants and the San Francisco 49ers' team chaplains, Pat Richie of the 49ers, and Dave Bratton of the Giants approached the Christian leaders of their teams. For the 49ers, Richie spoke with Brent Jones and Guy McIntyre. The chaplain wondered if there was something they could do or should do, as a reflection of their faith before an audience of 41.6 million viewers, a Monday Night Football record that still stands. Brent and Guy were all in.

It was a hard-fought defensive game with injuries and angry scuffles. A fracas between players ensued on the field at the end of the game, stealing the show and TV cameras didn't capture the Prayer Circle. As the last catch of the game was made and the 49ers won 7-3, Brent, Guy, Steve Wallace, Bubba Paris, Dave Waymer (now deceased) and Ron Lewis moved together, huddled up, took a knee and started to pray. Two Giants, Howard Cross and Reyna Thompson came running in to join the circle ten seconds after this photo was snapped, the only known photo of the circle.

The wheels were set in motion for a faith-based tradition that, at the time, some called "radical" but ultimately became prevalent around the NFL, college and high school ball and even some Pop Warner leagues.

Brent's comment on the Prayer Circle was pretty simple: "We were chosen to take a leap of faith, so we did." Both teams were threatened with $25,000 fines per player and a one million dollar fine for the owners, but no fines were ever officially called.

After retiring from the NFL in January 1999, the phone started ringing with calls for Brent from local and national politicians asking him to run for public office. It was a nice compliment to Brent's ethics and ability to effect change. The couple was flattered, but they got some advice from the great Steve Largent. His advice was that playing in the NFL was equal to living life in a frying pan. He said getting into politics is living life directly in the fire. He reminded them that their two girls were too young and that they need to consider the whole family. He said that becoming a politician will always be an option, but that they are Rachel and Courtney's mom and dad first and foremost. That was an aspect they hadn't really considered until hearing it from an NFL peer who had walked that very path.

Dana confides that one day, in the thick of being courted by the GOP, she was waiting for Brent to arrive at their daughter's junior high volleyball match:

"He arrived about ten minutes into the match, came up into the stands with a little sheepish grin and said 'I can explain,' to which I responded "Well, it must be good!" He waited for a break in the action and then leaned over and said 'I was on the phone with Newt.' I shifted my head for eye to eye, 'Newt who? Oh my! ... wait... *that* Newt? You're kidding!' I initially forgot to ask what he had to say. I truly was baffled that Newt Gingrich had Brent's cell phone number!

"Brent said that if the government wants to get ahold of you, they will and that Newt, who was then the Speaker of the House, had strongly suggested that Brent owed it to his country to come to Washington, stand on the steps of our nations' capital, spend a week with him to see how everything works; and then try and say no to him and the GOP. WOW, we were breathless! Need to pray about this!!!

"But with all that we had been through in the NFL, one thing we are very good at is keeping our heads on straight and not getting too enamored. Brent and I went back and forth, round and round on the possibility of diving head first into the political scene. Between Steve Largent's wise counsel, a conversation with J.C. Watts and Newt's invitation, even though our love of country is truly strong and unbreakable, at that particular time in our lives, after deep prayerful consideration, it was not the right time. Of course we want to make a difference, but God leads, and it did not feel right."

They declined all offers.

God opened another door almost immediately and showed Dana and Brent their next adventure- in the Big Apple! The family moved to New Canaan, Connecticut to work for CBS Sports in New York City. CBS had been out of telecasting NFL games for five years. For their entry back into the ratings race, they signed Jim Nantz as host, and Brent, George Seifert (Brent's former coach) and Marcus Allen as in-studio commentators.

Dana says, "Brent loved sharing his knowledge of the game and his sense of humor was a wonderful relief to the entire set crew. The four of them had impressive chemistry and even our girls got to know the crew well. However, when Brent was moved to broadcasting games, long weekends without seeing his family, lots of flying, back and forth, with the stress of new safety measures after 9/11, all took a toll."

The family moved back to the Bay Area, exactly 2.5 miles from the home they sold to move east, and returned to their beloved Community Presbyterian Church. Brent could concentrate on Northgate Capital, the investment firm he co-founded with a couple of former teammates in 2000. He serves as a Managing Director aligning start-ups with the premier venture capital firms of Silicon Valley. He is also a direct investor in several Silicon Valley start-ups.

Brent, Courtney, Dana and Rachel at the Bay Area Sports Hall of Fame induction ceremony.

Rachel has graduated from California Polytechnic State University with a degree in Business Administration from the Orfalea School of Business. She works in sales and marketing. Courtney graduated from the University of North Carolina, Chapel Hill, with a degree in Management in Society. She retired in February 2015 from women's pro soccer after three seasons, is currently the CEO of Sweat Cosmetics and was married to Corbin Louks in March 2016. They split their time between Montreal, Quebec, Canada where he plays football for the CFL Montreal Alouettes, and the states.

Both of the girls played Division One soccer. Rachel was goalie for Cal Poly for two seasons and went into a managerial role after sustaining multiple injuries. Courtney was a forward at UNC and was drafted into the Women's Professional Soccer League by the Boston Breakers in 2012.

Brent and Dana have experienced the highs and lows of being in the public eye. They speak with emotion about their deep devotion to each other and their gratitude to God for His mercy and blessing through it all.

Asked if she would do anything differently today, Dana responds, "I wouldn't change a thing!"

> Brent's life verse: *"Trust in the Lord with all your heart and lean not on your own understanding; in all ways acknowledge him and he will make straight your paths.* Prov 3.6 RSV

> Dana's life verse: *"For I know the plans I have for you, declares the Lord, plans to prosper you and not to harm you, plans to give you hope and a future."* Jer 29.11 RSV

What principles and values from this story are also foundational in your life?

From Dana _____

_____

From Brent _____

_____

SAM AND PEGGY CLARKE

Photo: Joel Sorrell

WHAT WILL YOUR LEGACY BE?

A PHILOSOPHER'S LEGACY

"I am a searcher of wisdom on the important things in life. I also search out the answers to very complex questions and condense explanations sufficient for the intelligent reader to understand the issues so they will no longer be fooled."

Sam Clarke describes himself as a learner, a thinker and frustrated teacher. Born in Wenatchee, Washington in 1929 during the Great Depression, he graduated from Bainbridge High School in 1948 and from the University of Washington, majoring in Psychology, then earned a Master's Degree in Exercise Physiology. Sam has had eight careers in business, academia, medicine, psychology, teaching, training, real estate and commercial land development. He is passionate about understanding the complex and vital issues affecting Americans today.

Like the great scholars and philosophers who have inspired him: Drucker, Schweitzer, Tolle, Freidman, Sowell and others, Sam exhaustively studies one vital issue at a time. Weighty issues indeed: Economics, energy, education, welfare, abortion, taxation, poverty, the environment, crime, civil morality, liberalism, conservatism, health care and others. He then condenses what he has learned from many respected sources into an easy-to-read several paragraphs on that subject. He shares them with friends, family and others who are interested.

Sam calls these gems *Tidbits* and hopes to publish them one day as a book. Another work underway is a book entitled *Vital Issues*, a more in depth examination of the issues facing America today. He says,

"The Tidbits contain not only research, but also timeless, common sense principles and ideas. Politics today operates commonly by deception, rather than the truth, so, based on research, experience and reflection, I tell people enough truth that they can vote intelligently. Valid writers think critically before they write. My study results in some wonderfully exciting 'Ah-Ha!' moments! Life has taught me many things I'd like to give away."

Sam's beloved wife, Margaret (known as Peggy) has stood with him through his quest for knowledge and enlightenment for 63 years. She says, "Sam is my teacher. My vocation is my family – teaching my children to become loving, caring people and to trust the Lord. Our six kids go to their dad on intellectual matters and come to me when they need a shoulder or have a problem."

Family is very important to Peggy. Born in 1931 in Kansas City, Missouri, she was adopted in September of that year, not knowing her biological parents. Her adoptive mother died when Peggy was three. Since her adoptive father was often hospitalized with heart problems, Peggy stayed in various foster homes. Her adoptive father died of a heart attack during their visit to his older brother's home in Seattle in 1939. Peggy was taken in by her father's older brother and his wife, who already had five children and two other family members.

Sam says of Peggy, "She is the world's quintessential mother. She thinks with her heart. It has taken me sixty years to learn how to be a good husband to her."

With all of his accrued knowledge and intellectual skills, Sam Clarke turns to mush and happy tears flow when he talks about their six accomplished children. Jeff is an internal medicine physician; Theresa and Colleen are marketing professionals; Denise is a para-educator working with developmentally-impaired; and Mike, an MBA graduate of the University of Washington, is a territory manager for business development. Their youngest child, Ed, also an MBA graduate, is a manager with Microsoft.

They are a close family. Sam beams when he describes their grandchildren as "charming in their imperfections." He and Peggy are now looking forward to the birth of their third grandchild.

The grandchildren are included in another of Sam's passions; mentoring and equipping young people. Sam, now retired, was president of the Success Foundation in North Kitsap which focused on recruiting citizens of the community to mentor kids in high schools.

Sam says, "There are lots of experienced and mature people out there in every community who can help. School systems tend to be insular and disinclined to think outside the box. They can be reluctant to allow the community in. This work, now assimilated by Bainbridge Youth Services, has shifted its focus to high school internships, involving many businesses in the County.

It's about control, but we are gradually making inroads with forward-thinking educators in Kitsap County. My own early life experiences have motivated me in this effort. I quit medical school after two years due to stress and lack of money. Nobody told me I had other options! Mentoring would have been a great help to me. We at the Foundation believe in the power of mentoring to help the youth of America."

Peggy has been a great support to Sam in his mentoring work, sitting in on sessions and offering her perspective as a mother, especially to kids who come from disadvantaged backgrounds. She says, "Once I was telling a young girl about our 6 children and 15 grandchildren. She was astonished and asked, 'Are they all from one dad?' Children today are hungry for someone to help them make sense of their circumstances and give them hope for the future. Many are not learning that at home."

Sam has worked cheerfully and tirelessly in his community in many other ways. He was the developer of the Bainbridge Island Racquet Club, Sterling Place Building and Central Market in Poulsbo, Washington. He was broker/owner of Real Estate Development

Systems, a commercial real estate firm. Years ago, Sam was invited to join the board of the Kitsap Community Foundation and devoted four years to helping drive their mission to serve all nonprofits within the County by gathering endowments for youth, education, the arts and social needs.

Sam and Peggy also operate their own family endowment fund which gifts to charitable organizations. "We give to charities that put people first. Things work or don't work because of the integrity of the people. If you don't have trust, you can't have collaboration. We support public policy organizations also. Without watchdogs, there is no compelling necessity for government to function well."

A testimonial to Peggy Clarke's mothering acumen and love was disclosed when the kids were growing up and finishing school. She drew one of her sons aside to say, "People ask me how come none of your children got into drugs or such trouble as that." Her son responded, "We couldn't have done anything like that, Mom, because we knew how much it would hurt you!"

Sam is completing a book; *Helping in a Heartfelt Way*, for those who would like to assist others who are living with stress or lacking understanding of their own potential. In other words, how to be truly helpful by drawing guidance from our essential self, our heart. His philosophy of life and exhaustive study of other great writers and philosophers over the centuries, has led him to share his wisdom. Here are a few tidbits from that book:

Helping:
"I believe that all of our encounters are ordained, and that we have the power and grace to cooperate with a healing effect. It requires, essentially, a presence of mind and courage of conviction that predisposes us to allow that enrichment to occur."

Truth:
"Only truth truly exists, and is eternally present whether we see it clearly or not."

Compassion:

"Our task is simply to engage with a brother with charity in our heart. We need to just do the work before us as best we can, and leave the rest to God."

Scholar, philosopher, business leader, mentor and seeker of truth, Sam Clarke, reminds us of a quote from philosopher/psychiatrist, Carl Jung who was asked whether he believed in God. Jung said, "No, I don't *believe* in God. I *know* there is God." Sam added, "Intellectual understanding and *truly knowing* are different. It is thrilling for Peggy and me to watch our children grow in knowledge and spiritual understanding. This is the only thing that will save the world today."

"A new commandment I give to you, that you love one another; even as I have loved you ... By this all men will know that you are my disciples, if you have love for one another." Jn 14.34,35 RSV

What principles and values from this story are also foundational in your life?

From Sam _____

_____

From Peggy _____

_____

BILL WEITZEL

Photo: Boaz Crawford

A LEGACY OF PERSEVERANCE

W e know that life has its peaks and valleys. It's great at the top of the mountain. But it is not easy to have clarity of vision and the fortitude to carry on under extreme stress and seemingly insurmountable adversity, and still be able to leave a legacy that is not only tangible, but also a triumph of the human spirit.

Bill Weitzel has been in deep valleys countless times in his remarkable life. His tenacity to keep coming back from daunting physical crises is astonishing.

At six months of age, Bill had a thyroid cyst in his neck removed surgically which left some paralysis on one side of his face. In that same year, 1928, he contracted polio and spent 7 of his first 11 years of life as a resident of Seattle Children's Orthopedic Hospital, then located in the Queen Ann area of Seattle.

The first iron lung was being tested in 1928 but was not available to many hospitals, so Bill was laid on his back on a half circle contraption built just for him which, it was hoped, would correct curvature of the spine. His head and his feet were below his stomach. He exercised daily to the playing of *"American Patrol"* by Glenn Miller.

With great sadness, Bill recalls. "When I was seven, I had seniority because I'd been living at the hospital longer than any of the many other kids who had polio, so I got a bed next to a window. One warm summer day, my window was open and I could hear a tin can being kicked up the street. The sound got closer and closer. From my bed, I could make out two boys about my age who were perched on the curb of the street below the window. They were griping that they hated summer because they had nothing to do and were bored, wishing school would start up again. I listened to them from my bed, welling up with frustration and wanting with all of my strength to shout, *'I wish I could kick a tin can up the street! I wish I could be down on that street!'* All I wanted in the world was to get out of that place and go to school and here's somebody who doesn't know what to do with himself when he can do anything he wants to do! I was depressed for months after that."

During those seven years in the polio ward, Bill also suffered a ruptured appendix. Then later, during adenoid surgery, a muscle was taken out, leaving him with a sagging shoulder and one arm longer than the other.

Teachers came to the hospital to school the children who had polio. According to Bill, "They said it was school, but the teachers felt such pity for us, they gave out good grades no matter how poorly we did. They meant well."

After time in a convalescent center, Bill was finally allowed to go home at age 11, with a back brace and one leg shorter than the other. He was placed in fifth grade at Lafayette, a public school in West Seattle, a dark time that he calls one of the bleakest periods of his life.

"I couldn't spell. I didn't know English sentence structure, math, or history," he laments. "I had none of the rudimentary early learning skills other children had experienced. So I taught myself, determined to do my best." I read books, I tried things, I found out that I could learn and actually make a life for myself! I taught myself, determined to do my best."

His best indeed!

Before graduating high school, Bill achieved Honor Society status, was captain of the debate team, vice president of the Boy's Club and editor of the school newspaper.

His journalism teacher called him one of the best editors she had ever had because he got the paper out on time every time. Bill learned that with hard work, organized planning and the courage to try, he could accomplish anything. And so he did.

During high school, Bill earned a dime for each prescription delivered for the local pharmacy and $20 a month from a paper route. He was able to buy a car and earned enough to enroll at the University of Washington in 1947. In his first year there, he saw a card notice pinned to the job bulletin board. A floor cleaning business was for sale, along with one floor waxing machine and three customers. Bill sold his car and bought the company for $350. His total income was $48 per month.

He says, "I was going to the University to learn how to make money and I was already making it! So, I quit school because I was getting more and more customers through word of mouth and was unable to keep up my studies."

Thus Dependable Building Maintenance Inc. became a reality in Seattle. It was destined to become one of the best companies of its kind in the years to come.

In his early 20's, Bill met Shirley, his wife of 45 years, and became the proud father of his two girls, Kerry and Tamar. Shirley was a great dancer. So was Bill! After his terrible start in life, he went home to parents who were dancers. Bill learned how to dance from his parents and he practiced with his sister.

"My wife, Shirley and I were regulars at places like the Trianon Ballroom and the Black & Tan Club on Madison," Bill says joyfully. "When we danced the Boogie Woogie and the Jitterbug, everyone else left the floor to watch us! We won trophies and had quite a reputation on the dancing circuit!"

In his early 60's, Bill was hit with yet another medical trial. Diagnosed with cancer of the esophagus, he nearly died. "The doctor botched the operation," he recalls. "He clipped my spleen, colon and pancreas removing the cancer. I needed 22 units of blood, was unconscious three days, in intensive care for 18 days and in the hospital 45 days. It took two years recovery time and I was left with weakness on my entire right side and a shortened rib cage. I know how worried my family was, but I survived!"

And, in over 50 years of Bill's leadership, Dependable Building Maintenance, Inc. also survived to become a multi-million dollar business. When Bill sold in 1994, it was one of the premier building maintenance companies in America with offices in over a dozen states, more than one thousand employees and franchises across the country.

As a successful businessman, Bill says he watched the deterioration of the unions.

"In the early days, the unions cared about their members who respected a good day's work," he says. "Over time, the union leadership became more left leaning, protecting themselves and using member dues for their own political purposes. I knew of one union boss who took three salaries: one from the local, one from the Western Conference and one from the International. And his yacht had a fireplace in it."

Asked how it was that he could persevere all of his nearly 89 years, Bill responded, "I am a very determined person, but I am careful what I pick to be determined about. I don't sweat the small stuff. Time is the most valuable asset I have. I try to use my time accordingly. Because I lost so much of my youth in hospitals, I didn't have a normal childhood. I determined that success was not only accomplishing something, but enjoying life. If you're not enjoying life every day, you are not successful."

For Bill Weitzel, enjoying life includes playing golf. In his 20's and 30's, Bill's handicap was seven. Smiling with his eyes, he says, "Today, I play golf in the winter in Palm Desert and at Overlake Golf Club in Medina. "But I don't talk about my handicap anymore.

> *"Be strong and of good courage, and do it. Fear*
> *not, be not dismayed: for the Lord God is with you.*
> *He will not fail you or forsake you ..."* 1 Chr
> 28.20 RSV

What principles and values from this story are also foundational in your own life?

From Bill _____

_____

DR. PETER W. SCHRAMM,
Executive Director of Ashbrook Center

AMERICA'S CONVERSATIONALIST

D
r. Peter Schramm is remembered by his students as a great teacher who loved books and loved to help students learn well and to challenge themselves; by his colleagues as one who put his heart and soul into the business of learning about the goodness and greatness of America and passing that learning on to whomever would listen; and by his friends as a devoted and passionate man who loved his country, who treasured friendship; a physically strong and imposing figure, but inside was a great heart.

Peter was born December 23, 1946 in Gyor, Hungary, son of William and Rose Anna Schramm. He and his family risked their lives fleeing communist Hungary in 1956 to come to America. Peter's father always told him, "We were born American, but in the wrong place." So, for his tenth birthday, his father gave him America.

Peter's family started Schramm's Hungarian Restaurant in Studio City, California where he worked as a waiter while attending high school and California State University Northridge. His love of books and learning led to a B.A. in History in 1971; an M.A. in Government from Claremont Graduate School in 1975; an M.A. in International History from the London School of Economics in 1976; and a Ph.D. in Government from Claremont Graduate School in 1980.

Out of gratitude for the freedom that had been given to him, and love for all that was worthy of love in his adopted country, Peter devoted his life to studying and teaching the principles of American freedom.

He was the founding President of the Claremont Institute for the Study of Statesmanship and Political Philosophy, whose mission is to restore the principles of the American Founding to their rightful place in American life. He served in the Reagan Administration as Director of the Center for International Education in the United States Department of Education. He served from 1987 as Director, Executive Director, then Senior Fellow of the Ashbrook Center at Ashland University in Ohio, whose mission it is to restore and strengthen the capacities of the American people for constitutional self-government and the virtues required of a free people.

As a full professor at Ashland University and Director of the Ashbrook Scholar Program, Peter was a beloved teacher to generations of students. His dear wife, Sally, cherishes his memory, remembering his laugh, which was "that great American laugh; loud, clear and true."

Peter passed away August 16, 2015. Five weeks before his death, more than 700 friends, colleagues and former students gathered at Ashbrook to celebrate this great man. Speakers included notable scholars, colleagues and close friends including Dr. Larry Arnn, President of Hillsdale College; Bill Kristol, political analyst and founder of The Weekly Standard and Jonah Goldberg, conservative syndicated columnist, author, commentator and Senior Editor of National Review.

The event was a mix of a good-hearted "roast" and heartfelt testimonials to the greatness of this good man. At the end of the celebration, Peter took the stage to an extended ovation from the crowd and with a mighty effort, spoke of his happiness and gratitude. His farewell touched the hearts of all in attendance and those who have watched the video of the event. His devoted wife writes this tribute to her husband:

"Peter was the best of men. He was honorable, courageous, thoughtful, and ever purposeful. Never was another more generous.

With a fine mind and a big heart, he argued with manly eloquence in favor of all that is good and true and beautiful. He was a gentleman, an American gentleman. He not only loved his country but knew why it was worth loving, and he taught us why this is so. Peter loved life and lived fully. He was the rarest soul I ever knew. His great soul was a joy to be with, and he made everyone around him better. He made me better. He was my poet, my best beloved. And my heart overflows with gratitude for our beautiful gift of days." Sally J. Schramm

One of Peter's great quotes is: "In America, each generation has to be educated in our principles of right, the natural rights that stem from those principles, and about our constitutional soul, which gives these rights their functional order. As Madison put it, 'liberty and learning always have to be attached.' In this unique country— this *novus ordo seclorum*—citizens have to be made because it is not enough that they be born. —PWS"

Peter Schramm was a great-souled man, with a love for life and learning that was contagious. He enlisted everyone he met in the joyous pursuit of all that is good and beautiful and true about America. I urge you to research his writings and continue the legacy of his conversation about the land he loved and why.

Here is one sample of Peter's countless writings: this one from *On Principles*, published by Ashbrook Center May 2003:

The Ugly European

I lived in Munich in 1968. This was my first trip to Europe since leaving it at age ten. My reason for going was to learn German. My reason for staying was to learn something about Europeans, their habits and their ways, and their rich history. In the end, I learned a great deal about how Europeans see America, and therefore learned much about why I love Americans. But above all, I learned much about Europeans.

What I learned then has remained true, and helps explain some of the French and German shenanigans over Iraq. The French power play that we have been witnessing over the past few months is only partly a reflection of disagreements over Iraq specifically, and American foreign policy generally. It is certainly an attempt by the French to break the American monopoly of power in the world. Although it is geopolitics of the highest sort, it is also and more importantly, a reflection of different dispositions, of different intellectual and moral habits. Europeans note our power and wealth, but have contempt for (what they see as) our ignorance. These two things combine into resentment. And that resentment is fed by a deep well of continental philosophy, a view of the world that Americans don't share. And this is the crux of the matter.

It was a tough and lonely year. At age twenty-two I enrolled at the University of Munich to better my German (and to sit in on some philosophy seminars). Since I had about seventy-five bucks in my pocket when I arrived, I needed a job. I got one through the only friend I had there (a Hungarian poet-in-exile) and I was able to stay. The job was ridiculously difficult. I worked twelve hour-days, six days a week, and was paid seventy-five cents an hour. But this paid for my room in a pension (two bucks a day) and I got to eat for nothing since I worked at the main market in Munich unpacking bananas from freight cars. The bananas were free, and the owner only charged fifteen cents for soft drinks or a beer.

The job wasn't legal, of course. They called it "black" labor; it was off the record, I was paid in cash. I was hired only because I didn't tell them I was an American student; they never would have hired me. I told them I was a Hungarian refugee. They were willing to help. My fellow laborers were bums, German bums (we would call them homeless now). Although they smelled awful, drank too much and slept on park benches, I liked them. I became especially fond of them when I finally figured out what they were humming as we worked. They were singing and humming American songs, old songs, like "The Yellow Rose of Texas."

After a few weeks of working with them I got to know them well enough to ask them how it was that they were singing American songs. Well, it turned out that they had been soldiers in World War

II and were among the first Germans captured by the Americans. They were sent to a prisoner of war camp in Texas. They lived out the whole war in Texas, they learned English and liked our songs. And because this was an American prisoner of war camp, they were able to leave the camp, get jobs in town and got acquainted with real Americans. All four of them said it was the best experience of their lives. They loved Americans, they said.

I wanted to know what it was they liked about Americans. They thought that Americans were direct and honest. They looked you square between the eyes and told you what they thought. The Americans laughed a lot, often loudly. Their view of life was not tragic, they were not filled with the passionate anxiety of Europeans. Americans had no angst. They didn't spend their time regretting the past; they thought anything was possible. Give a man an opportunity, he'll take it, and fulfill what ambitions he had. My German friends called this "practical freedom." These Americans lived as free men should live. They were modest, never overbearing, and gave no quarter to flim-flam. And they were very generous. Although we were soldiers for a country that they were at war with, the Germans explained, the Americans never said they disliked Germans. They did keep asking us, however, how we could have gotten ourselves a leader like the one we had. It started us thinking, they said.

Everybody in America seemed young, they said. They had a liveliness about them, a kind of wide-eyed-adolescence, as if they had never experienced disappointment and defeat, and there was no reason to think they ever would. They were energetic and full of vigor. They thought that people should have the opportunity to excel in something. These Americans moved through the world as if there was no one trying to hinder their progress, their ambition, their way in the world. The Germans said that they were struck by the fact that the children seemed to look mature men in the eyes, as if they were their equals.

We talked about these matters in my halting German. And after a while, I felt morally compelled to tell them that I was really an American and that I spoke English. Well, you should have seen the hurrahs and the cheer! They were delighted and quickly revealed that their English was much better than my German. From then on we spoke only English.

Over the years, and on other trips, much was added to this opinion. Although none denied what my homeless friends understood to be the American character, they added some not so subtle mixes to that opinion. What had been described as virtues now became vices. Many Frenchmen I met argued that Americans were money grubbing, all they were interested in was making money. The country was full of an endless commercial bustle. As a result Americans worked too hard, and had no proper understanding of leisure. Their culture was minimal and only their manners were lower. They were unsophisticated and un-learned, they knew little about their own history, and nothing about the history of others. They had never suffered, so they lacked depth. That may explain why they had no great literature and why were not in love with museums, as Europeans were.

I remember one man who couldn't possibly understand how all these people of different backgrounds and colors could live together as something like citizens; he wondered how it was possible. He concluded — because he never understood its cause, the idea, the electric cord, as Lincoln called it, that was the real basis of American patriotism — that it was not possible in the end, that it was only a question of time before the place fell apart. Not enough ties of blood, not enough common history, he said.

In the end I came to learn that what held together all the critical opinions about America was the spirit of resentment and envy. We were big and powerful and thought we were special. We claimed to establish a novus ordo seclorum (see the Great Seal of the United States on the back of the dollar bill), as if we had reinvented the world. We scoffed at the old and tired ways of the mother continent, we were like children who weren't able to appreciate the sober and cultured ways of the parents. These European parents were jealous of their energetic and ambition children. The child became too powerful, too wealthy, too ambitious. The more the child was able and willing to help the parents out, the more resentful the parents became. And yet, the parents were forced to admit to themselves that there was something especially interesting and appealing in these exuberant youths, their liveliness and their straight-shooting ways. And yet again, these youngsters had to be kept in check by their betters.

Over the years I began to see the philosophical basis of their thinking, and why they disliked our ways. They attempted to prove that all philosophical questions and human life can be reduced to the deep Grundproblemen (fundamental problems) and then to nihilistic despair, because in becoming fully enlightened the Europeans freed themselves from all illusions about good and evil, and right and wrong. But we Americans didn't think this and we couldn't feel the despair. How could we simple-minded and practical folk understand the depth of the human condition? We Americans insist on holding to the connection between freedom and justice, courage and moderation. As a result, we couldn't take the Europeans as seriously as they took themselves. We thought that they were participants in a sophisticated and endless coffee-house chatter leading nowhere except the will to power and gulags and concentration camps. We, on the other hand, thought that equality and liberty had ethical and political implications; we were willing to fight to make men free.

It should not surprise us that the Old Europeans have been taking advantage of our current situation (the war on terrorism and Iraq) to try to revivify their worn down power in the world, and their old grandeur. The post September 11 world is the first true international crisis in a world now dominated by American power. The Iraq problem has given the Old Europeans an opportunity to try a dangerous gambit. They tried to challenge the legitimacy of American power, and they failed, as they have failed in their philosophical instructions to us. We are still optimists who laugh too loudly, and we still think, along with Mark Twain, that against the assault of laughter, nothing can stand. Peter W. Schramm, Executive Director of the Ashbrook Center.

Professor Peter W. Schramm

"For the Lord will not forsake his people; he will not abandon his heritage; for justice will return to the righteous, and all the upright in heart will follow it."
Ps 94.14,15 RSV

What principles and values from this story are also functional in your life?

From Peter _____

_____

CHIE MENDOZA, CAREGIVER

THE CAREGIVER'S LEGACY

W e know that America's older citizens are living longer, due to medical advances, changes in diet, exercise and staying active. For many, though, Alzheimer's disease and Dementia have forever changed their happy lives into a time referred to as the "Long Goodbye."

Alzheimer's Dementia (AD) is the most common and best known cause of dementia. It is defined as a progressive disease that slowly changes the chemistry and structure of the brain, leading to the death of brain cells. Confusion, forgetfulness and mood swings are common and lead to memory loss and lack of communication skills.

Once diagnosed, the family faces the issue of how to take care of their loved one. In many cases, the spouse has unknowingly become the caregiver as a husband or wife slowly begins to exhibit some of the symptoms. The tipping point for urgency of finding care comes after a "final" fall that lands a loved one in the hospital or it may come as a violent outburst or signs of depression so deep it can devastate family relationships.

When you know what it is and fully accept that you can't care for your loved one by yourself, who can you trust to take the same care of your loved one as you would at home? Depending on the prescribed level of care, Adult Family Homes for Dementia are a good alternative to institutional care.

Chie Mendoza is the owner of four AFH homes for Dementia. They are called Homecomings 1, 2, 3 and 4. Chie was born in Santiago Old Nabua, Camarines Sur Philippines. The Filipino people are known for their devotion to family and their dedication to caring for the elderly. Chie was raised by a nurturing mother and dad and says, "My heritage is important to me. My family is my first love and my everything."

In the Philippines, Chie graduated from Nabua National High School and studied Accounting at Divine Word College of Legazpi where she earned a Bachelor of Science in Commerce degree in Accounting in 1992. She came to the United States in 1999, is married and has a 17-year-old daughter. Her husband is a businessman but is also very supportive of Chie's work.

And that work is not easy. This energetic, always happy person travels in her car daily between her four homes, bringing good cheer to residents, confirming their good health and delivering fresh groceries and treats. The residents love to see her coming. One said, "She lights up a room with her smile!" One of the Filipino staff was a chef in the Philippines, so meals are nutritious and appropriate for each resident.

Chie's first job in America was part time caregiver in an adult family home. "It was a very hard job," she says. "I learned the fundamentals of caring for Dementia patients. I am a fast learner and whatever my boss gave to me, I grabbed it. My supervisor praised me, telling me my smile and happy attitude helps them to live. I cried if I made a mistake.

"One day a resident wandered and left the premises. I wanted to die, I was so scared. I ran around the neighborhood without my shoes. I am running and calling his name and thanks be to God, I found him two blocks away. He was confused. I held his hand and asked him which way he is going and he answered 'to my home.' So, I told him I will help him find it and we peacefully walked back home to safety. That was a great lesson for me, never to happen again.

"I became more attentive and broadened my experiences and training and knew that one day, I would own a home like this and bring loving care to these dear people who I love and respect."

Chie was licensed and opened her first AFH fourteen years ago, working very hard as the only employee for the first year in order to pay off startup loans. Then she began hiring qualified staff, saying "Thanks be to God that I didn't get discouraged with all the work. I have high standards for myself. Staff must be honest with me because I know each one of my residents, their families, their medication needs and am a hands-on boss. I like to go to the grocery store and buy special foods for them that keep them happy and healthy. I monitor my residents and staff every day."

Three years later, Homecomings 2 opened, then 3 and 4. Medical professionals and physical therapy helpers visit the homes. In a rare health emergency, Chie is known by local hospitals for her visits to her residents who have short hospital stays. There, too, she lights up the room with her smile until her resident comes back home.

Chie offers this advice: "Finding the right place for a loved one is difficult. The first step is determining what level of care is needed; skilled nursing that provides for 24/7 medical needs or home care for environmental assistance with daily living like bathing, grooming, dressing, eating and restroom needs. Home care includes supervision and monitoring of medication administration, serving nutritious meals and a well-trained staff for special needs.

"Dementia is a dreaded and progressive condition for residents. There is no treatment or cure for it. All we can do is continue supporting and understanding them, giving them the quality of life they deserve. Adult Family Homes are regulated by the State Department of Health and Human Services, making sure we follow the rules and regulations for care of the elderly. Inspections and investigations are fair and important to put an end to homes that do not follow the rules."

Chie sings and prays with her residents. She says, "God always comes first. He is always my Guide and protects me as His child. My prayer every morning is 'Bring me word of your unfailing love, for I have put my trust in You. Show me the way I should go, for to You I entrust my life and my work.'"

Chie says taking care of Dementia residents is not only stressful. It is fun. They laugh a lot. One 87 year-old resident loves to play with his food at dinner. He forms his mashed potatoes like a mountain and makes a hole in the middle, then pours his juice on top of it. He says it is his volcano. Another was a registered nurse in her career and a social worker. She is mobile and thinks she works as the lead RN in the home. She bosses the caregivers and fires them if they are not doing their job well. One day, she fired Chie!

There is a resident hoarder who loves collecting stuff. One day the daughter of a resident came to visit her mother. She left her shoes by the door and when she came to get her shoes, they were not there. Staff searched high and low but couldn't find them anywhere. The daughter ended up wearing a pair of her mother's shoes to go back home. Staff found the daughter's shoes in the morning, securely wrapped in the hoarder's dresser drawer.

A good sense of humor is helpful to reduce stress and create empathy in social situations and it helps some to cope with pain. Pain and loss are the obstacles to quality of life for the Dementia resident.

Let us thank God for caregivers like Chie Mendoza.

> *"Do not rebuke an older man, but exhort him as you would a father; treat younger men like brothers, older women like mothers, younger women like sisters, in all purity. Honor the widows."* 1 Tim 5.1-3 RSV

What principles and values from this story are also foundational in your life?

From Chie _____

_____

TRISH AND DR. BOB JANKELSON

Photo by Joel Sorrell

THE LEGACY OF A RENAISSANCE MAN

"Life is a blank canvas on which to paint a new masterpiece every day. Your palette is joy and opportunity. Blend the palette. Create a masterpiece that you can share with friends, family and loved ones. Don't waste it. Make broad brush strokes of love, generosity, compassion, and stewardship."
Dr. Bob Jankelson

Bob Jankelson is often referred to as a Renaissance man. He is a retired dental clinician, renowned medical researcher, a farmer, patriot, visionary, and an entrepreneur who thinks with his heart as well as his inquisitive mind.

Born in Seattle, Bob and his twin brother were raised by their grandmother on the same family homestead farm where she was born in Washington Territory just prior to statehood in 1889. Bob says, "My grandmother stepped forward when our mother became afflicted with multiple sclerosis when we were very young. My grandmother was a woman with the most noble of human traits, who taught us the joy and dignity of hard work and the difference between needs and wants. She asked for nothing and gave everything.

"Life on the farm meant milking, haying, hoeing, raising chickens, growing virtually all of our own produce, chopping wood for the kitchen range, and drawing water from the well since we didn't have running water until 1951. That work ethic was our foundation for success in later life.

In the 1940's, little was known about multiple sclerosis, so while "Granny" raised the twins, Bob's father, Dr. Bernard Jankelson, began a quest to discover what had afflicted his beloved wife. Working in the departments of biophysics at the University of Washington and Oregon Schools of Medicine, he built a strong reputation in the study of neuromuscular problems of the head and neck and became internationally-known as a pioneer and expert in neuromuscular studies of jaw function.

Upon graduation in 1963 from the U of W Dental School, Bob teamed with his famous father to continue pioneering neuromuscular studies of jaw/facial/cervical muscle pathology and dysfunction. They worked closely together to develop groundbreaking technologies for diagnosis and treatment of temporomandibular disorders and other head and neck dysfunctions. Both were widely recognized and honored for their professional contributions. In 1990, Bob authored a textbook which is still widely used in the profession and is referred to as the reference "bible" on the subject.

Bob says of his father, "He was a brilliant, iconoclastic individual, born in South Africa, raised in Saskatchewan, educated at the University of Oregon. It was serendipitous that I could enter professional life with him. Our relationship was a symbiosis that benefited patients around the world. I give this advice to young doctors following in their fathers' footsteps: 'Always listen to every word your father says, but never, ever, ever let him know you are listening.' It worked for me."

For 40 years, Bob has shared his scientific expertise, teaching around the world, including 88 world lecture tours to Italy, Japan, England, France, Spain, Brazil, and Argentina. He moved to Chelan, Washington in 1994, intending to keep a low profile. Little did he know that one day he would go back to farming.

In 1999, apple growers in Eastern Washington were in severe distress due to an Alar scare and foreign competition, so Bob bought up several large orchards with a passion to preserve the agricultural legacy of the Chelan Valley.

Then, the thinker thought "If this land can grow some of the world's best apples, why not grapes?" Already an admirer of Italian culture, honed by 40 teaching trips to Italy, Bob learned everything he could about wine. "I have a relatively pedestrian palate," he says. "I believe there are two kinds of wine. Those you like and those you don't."

In his extensive travels, it was Italy that captured Bob's heart. His love of Italian culture and his passion for things Italian are evident in the architecture and operation of Tsillan Cellars Winery, known as the crown jewel of the sixteen wineries in the area. The name reflects the Indian spelling for Chelan. Tsillan Cellars is situated on a sloping knoll on Highway 97A, with a breathtaking view of the mountains, water and gardens of some of the finest grapes in the world.

Inspired by 15th century Italian architecture, Bob designed the architectural components of Tsillan Cellars and Sorrento's Ristorante. Referring to himself as a "Paper Napkin Architect," he recently designed and built a restaurant and event facility to best compliment the spectacular scenery of Lake Chelan and the North Cascade Mountains. He refers to it as his glass house inside an Italian gift box. With dramatic folding walls that open completely to the outdoors for the summer season, Sorrento's Ristorante was recently selected as one of America's top 100 scenic restaurants by Open Table guests.

Realizing that time and good health are continued blessings needed to complete his "dream" bucket list, Bob next designed an Italianate tasting room in Woodinville, Washington, which opened to rave reviews in early 2017.

The dreamer dreams on. The next and last dream on his bucket list is an Italian destination spa resort on his property adjacent to the winery and restaurant.

Bob Jankelson's Renaissance life has resulted in a multi-faceted legacy that will live forever. Now, if only he had a mate with whom he could share this great life.

Enter Trish.

Born in Lancashire, England, Trish arrived in Chelan to visit relatives in September 2008. She and Bob met at Tsillan Cellars during a Republican event honoring our country.

Trish's unique resume' includes living in Libya in 1969 when Qadaffi seized power. She lived in Rhodesia during the war years of the 1970s, returned to England in the 1980s. In 2000, Trish returned to Zimbabwe, the former Rhodesia, to become personal assistant for a "well-placed family" until shortly before her life-changing trip to Lake Chelan. In a joyous celebration, Bob and Trish were married on October 3, 2010.

Having lived under socialist and totalitarian governments, Trish joins Bob in his concern about the direction of America today. The patriot says, "The progressive notion of entitlement is debilitating and destroys the joy of work, the spirit of striving and accomplishment. Two pieces of paper; the Constitution and the Bill of Rights separate us from other world governments."

Bob says of Trish: "Being concerned about the 'coarsening' of American society, I appreciate the qualities Trish brings to my life; qualities that America should rediscover. She is always dressed impeccably even when working in the garden, the table is set with crystal and she takes a great deal of pride preparing a meal for us or for many. We try very hard to please each other. If we, as a society, made more effort to carry ourselves with dignity and uplift each other, we would be a better country. Trish is the perfect model."

In her delightful British accent, Trish says of Bob, "He functions at a different level than most people. However, he denies vehemently that he is different. He always tries to be kind, to be a good person, to do good deeds and share his good fortunes. I believe in the people of America and my husband is my best example."

The Renaissance man chimes in with, "I just want to be half the person that my dog, Rosie, thinks I am."

Bob has looked back eight decades in the rear view mirror bringing a flood of contemplative insights to share with us. Here are just a few:

THE GIFT: The chance that your parent's double helix genetic codes combined to create a healthy, sentient human life in the form of you, is greater than winning the national lottery. YOU WON! Your task is to take that Divine win, invest it wisely and leave your fellow man richer for your existence. Family, friends and strangers passing through our lives are to be mixed with love, joy, happiness, stirred with exuberance and humility. Create daily masterpieces of LIVING art. You do not know how many canvases will be allotted. Do not waste a canvas.

SUCCESS: Passion, vision, execution and perseverance are the four keystones to success. From childhood we all have varying degrees of passion, hope and dreams of what we think can be our destiny. All too often, the passion and vision of our early years do not come to fruition because we choose not to undertake the often difficult process of overcoming hurdles necessary to make our dreams reality. Success usually requires pick and shovel labor in the trenches. Perseverance is the ability to continue working in the trenches when others would quit in despair. The world is full of dreamers. Not so common is the dreamer who is a doer.

SHARING: The path to a noble life is often a tortuous, convoluted journey from the natural self-indulgence of our youth to the understanding that our greatest gift is our ability to share and uplift our fellow man. When hard work and serendipitous good fortune bestows success beyond your needs, seek good causes to share that good fortune. When advice is invited, share your wisdom with humility and sincere concern.

HEALTH: The old saw that "If you have your health, you have everything" may appear trite in the face of inevitable financial, educational, family, relationship and other stresses that are part of normal life. My professional career in practice and research has kept me in awe of the miracle of the functioning human body. The surprise is not that we are visited by so many barriers to healthy function, but that anything works. The complexity of the human brain should instill awe. The determination of the human heart should command respect. The less glamorous vital organs such as the kidneys, lungs and that great filter, the liver, are faithful bioengineering marvels. The millions of biochemical processes necessary to sustain human life are beyond comprehension. The inevitable decline of physical capabilities is transcended by the wisdom of age. We learn to find joy in life with the realization that we will maximize the physical and mental faculties granted us this day.

> *"Freedom is the foundation for human dignity and dignity is essential for elevation of the individual to reach their full potential."*
> Dr. Bob and Trish Jankelson

What principles and values from this story are also foundational in your life?

From Bob _____

_____

From Trish _____

_____

MATTHEW, BRIANNA, ERICA,
LAUREL AND SCOTT

A FAMILY LEGACY OF PRAYER

S cott and Laurel Christiansen take very seriously the slogan "The family that prays together, stays together." During their 36-year marriage, prayer as a family has been their steadfast commitment, through the highs and lows of daily life.

Laurel says, "Our parents were real Christians. It mattered deeply to them that their kids loved God. My two brothers and I listened to our parents pray on their knees by their bed every night and we all heard our names as they prayed for us. They were always sincere. Their walk with God mirrored their words and actions.

"My mom's family was large and very loving. My dad's father, an alcoholic, deserted his wife and four small boys. That's why my dad never drank alcohol. He had some sad stories to tell about his childhood. God changed my dad's life and gave him his dream of having a loving family."

Laurel and Scott met the last week of college before graduation from Washington State University. He was a Young Life Leader and Laurel was a leader in the Fellowship of Christian Athletes. Sadly, her Dad was diagnosed with cancer and passed away right after Scott proposed and asked her Dad for permission to marry his daughter. Laurel thinks that without a doubt God let her Dad know that Scott was the best choice and the Lord's choice for me.

Scott added to his B.A. from WSU a Computer Science degree from Seattle Pacific University, then an M.B.A. from SPU. He is Senior Manager in charge of the e-mail system for a major airplane company.

During and after college, Laurel worked until their first daughter, Erica was born and Laurel dove into the political arena, saying she got fed up with some behavior in the Clinton White House and called the Republican Party. Since then, she has been a driving force behind conservative candidates for public office in her home area.

The Christiansen family's example for prayerful living was their tiny church which had a group of prayer warriors that included her Mom and Aunts Esther, Charlotte and Laura. They lived close to each other and prayed for hours at a time. Scott learned quickly that if you needed prayer, go to them because they were considered to have a "direct line." Laurel's mom is now the only one left at age 98 and still a devout prayer warrior.

Laurel says, "Scott is a selfless person. The kids and I know that we always come first with Scott, after God. I hear him whisper, 'Thank you, Lord' when he wakes up in the morning. When Brianna and Matthew were born, I knew that, just like he did for Erica, Scott would be on his knees for them for all of their lives."

Scott prays with each of the children. It's a short "Dad" prayer during a hectic day and before bed. He puts his hand on each head as he prays. They stay perfectly still for the prayers and undoubtedly thank God silently for their loving father. They pray in the car when heading for school. That started when Dr. James Dobson said to pray for your kids on the way to school. "Well, I was always late, Laurel confesses, "and sometimes the prayer ended up being on the garage step and lasted 30 seconds. So, I started praying *with* them on the way to school.

Erica, age 28, is a software engineer working on developing new plane simulators. She has a degree in Electrical Engineering from SPU, interned at the National GeoSpatial Intelligence Agency where she had a very high security clearance at age 19. She worked for Northrop Grumman on their Hale Global Hawk Program. The

Hawk is an unmanned drone, the size of a Boeing 737. It gathers surveillance for our government and saves lives.

Matthew is the middle child. According to his mom, "He is our 'spark plug' always positive, never holds a grudge or sees ill in anyone. He tries to understand why people do what they do and is always forgiving. He makes us laugh. We are complete when Matthew is with us. He just graduated from Seattle Pacific University with an Electrical Engineering degree and is looking for a job.

Brianna was an answer to prayer. That's why her middle name is Joy. Erica always wanted a little sister. Scott and Laurel were going to adopt after four years of infertility drugs and doctors. Then Brianna was born. God heard their prayers!

Brianna spent the last two years of high school reading completely through the Bible and studied to understand it. She was a varsity golfer, ran track, played basketball and sang with the Revelation Choir in school. Her real love is robotics.

When she was 16, Bri witnessed some dangerous streets that little children had to cross to get to school. So, Bri, her Dad and her siblings, built a high tech robot to help children at school crossings. They asked for and received a Patent on their invention called *SafeTBot* and today are working on the 3rd prototype, intending to produce, manufacture and market their robot to schools, construction areas and places where vehicles and pedestrians meet. Brianna starts college in the fall with a $20,000 FIRST ever Robotics Scholarship, a $5,000 electrical engineering scholarship and a $1,500 Mechanical Engineering scholarship to SPU, hoping to make her dreams come true.

This family goes to prayer on issues large and small. Laurel tells the story of wanting to buy a car:

"We found a really cool Datsun 360Z, a two-seater and thought we would make an offer. Getting ready to go to the dealership, we stopped to kneel by our bed and both of us totally laid that car before God, saying, 'If it isn't your best, don't let us buy it.' We left it in His hands.

"At the dealership, we gave them a check and all of a sudden, I knew in my heart we should not buy the car. I looked at Scott and said, 'Get the money back. I don't feel good about this.' He said, 'I feel the same way.' He got the check and we left. Since that time, we always lay choices in our lives before God and let Him lead. The next day, we bought a Toyota Celica that lasted us through two kids and was an amazing car. God always seems to have better plans."

When the Christiansen family has a challenge or a crisis, they always start with prayer as a family. "We include the kids in prayer in tough times. Kids need to be prepared to face problems and there is no better way than watching and learning what their parents face. We pray first, then use our brains to handle the problem logically and forthrightly. Matthew, our forgiving child, is kind and compassionate. After the fact, we have heard amazing stories of Matthew standing up for someone who had been belittled by parents who made less than educated judgment calls. Matt is like his Dad.

"One day, we were packed and ready for a trip to Disneyland and the kids were so excited! Scott checked in at his office knowing that his employees were being evaluated and he just needed to see how things were going. This was a new group and one of them was being laid off. Scott had gotten to know the man about to be laid off and concluded there was no way this should happen because he was an excellent employee. Besides, Scott had learned that his wife had terminal cancer and needed the company benefits.

'I saw the kids sit down on the sofa. They were extremely quiet.

'For the next three hours, Scott fought to save the man's job. He did and we all celebrated.

"We asked Scott if he was going to tell the man what he had done and Scott said, 'No, it would crush him if he thought his employer did not appreciate his hard work and expertise. The man and his daughter enjoyed two more years with their wife and mother before she died. Scott went to the funeral. The Disneyland trip was delayed. It is good for children to experience such things. They grow in wisdom."

The Christiansen's love God's Word, especially Proverbs. Laurel says "Proverbs says it all! A favorite verse is *"Do not withhold good to them that it is due if it is in the power of your hand to give it."* That's why they try never to pass by a soldier without telling him or her of their heartfelt gratitude for their service and sacrifice for our freedom.

Laurel expresses deep concern for what is happening in our culture to so many of America's youth. "Especially to less fortunate kids," she says, "And it won't get better until our people ask God back into their lives and begin to work out the serious reasons for the appalling statistics in education, gang activity and poverty. We pray for revival and that God's love is revealed through His Holy Spirit to those who are hurting; and that we will see those who preach that good is evil and evil is good lose their influence and following."

She has this word for worried parents: "Follow the Word of God; study it, live by it, test everything by it. Pray together and wisdom will come. Let God's Spirit bring you peace and guidance. We know it works. You will know it, too."

> *"Trust in the Lord with all your heart, and lean not on your own understanding, in all your ways acknowledge him and he will direct your paths."*
> Prov 3. 5,6 RSV

What principles and values from this story are also foundational in your life?

From Scott _____

_____

From Laurel _____

_____

From the children _____

_____

171

YOUR ARTIST, RUTH MAYER

WHAT WILL YOUR LEGACY BE?

AMERICAN MASTER, RUTH MAYER

For years in the mid to late 1960's, I stood next to a red-headed girl with a beautiful smile in the second soprano section of our Lutheran church choir. Ruth Mayer had a small artist's studio in the area and was just starting out. Ruth had donated an original painting to the church which hung on the wall of the staircase to the upper rooms. As her friend, I knew that her art was the focus of her life. For years, I told her that one day she would be famous. I had no idea *how* famous.

Life went on and I did not see my friend, Ruth, for over two decades. Then, I read a piece in a magazine about an artist whose paintings of world-famous cityscapes were noted. There was a small photo of the artist, with long red hair and a beautiful smile. I located her and renewed our friendship.

Ruth Mayer's 60-year career has taken her to distant places on the globe, painting hundreds of works, including commissions from heads of state from countries around the world. She describes herself as an "Artist by Birth." She is known for her multitudes of painting styles. Visitors to her galleries are startled to learn the body of work of just one artist ranging from giant Cityscapes, Portraits, Surrealism, Realism, Abstracts, Impressionism, Fantasy, Landscapes, Seascapes, Sports … her repertoire is virtually limitless.

173

Among her many honors of distinction is the prestigious *"American Masters"* award from the Hubbard Museum in 1991. She also received a Key to the City of Las Vegas from the Mayor's office for her eight-foot painting, *"Las Vegas,"* which sold for $100,000 in 1985. Her 1997 painting, *"Hong Kong"* is described as a "Fait Accompli," celebrating Hong Kong's sovereignty.

"I Love New York" in 2000 shows the *"Great Angel"* embracing the sky behind the twin towers of the World Trade Center, a prophetic vision. The painting became a national monument to innocence everlasting; the same innocence of spirit in which it was painted.

A priest, inspired by the work *"I Love New York"* called Ruth to say, "We have traveled from Rome, representing the Vatican. We have been directed by God to have you paint Pope John Paul II. Will you accept the Commission to paint His Holiness?" The finished painting was unveiled for the Pope John Paul II on November 20, 2004.

Pope John Paul II and Ruth Mayer

Pope John Paul II greeted Ruth with a big smile, recognizing her as she entered the Great Room from his previous meetings with her many months prior. He laughed with her as she showed him in the painting as a boy and as a babe in his mother's arms. He rewarded her with a Blessing, and a thumbs up! The painting was dedicated to raising funds for children most in need.

Her painting, *"Tournament of Roses"* was commissioned by the Pasadena Tournament of Roses event, celebrating the oldest parade tradition in American history. The painting took three years to complete. Later, Ruth was commissioned by the Distinguished Flying Cross Society to paint *"The Distinguished Flying Cross,"* commemorating those who place themselves in harm's way that others may have the gift of life. The work resides in the San Diego Air and Space Museum, a branch of the Smithsonian Institute.

Ruth visited the Middle East in 2000 and experienced a barrage of emotions, saying; "It was history upon history, it was stones upon stones upon stones ... the place of the Story of stories." Her painting, *Jerusalem*, was seven years in progress.

Among signature characteristics of her work, Ruth paints herself in her paintings. You have to look very hard to find her. Look for her red hair in the flowers, the trees, the waters or the stones. There are "hidden" images of children in the clouds and in the sky and water. She says, "You never know when Angels are looking upon you." Ruth has never lost her childlike nature.

Ice Cream Girl   Ice Cream Boy

by Ruth Mayer

Children have always been a delight in Ruth's life. They are her other passion. She raised nine, including those she adopted. Children are an endless story in her art. As a child, she was raised on her father's fourteen thousand acre ranch in the Black Hills of South Dakota. She loved to ride bareback, standing on the horse's back while it galloped like the wind. You can feel the wind in your face in her paintings. Visitors to her father's ranch included Robert Frost, Dwight Eisenhower and she went to bull fights with her father and Pablo Picasso. The colorful cast in those times of her youth carved their memories in the vivid imagination of the young artist, Ruth Mayer.

An inner light has always shown in Ruth's work. Many have remarked, "I wonder if she uses something to make her paint glow," which, to Ruth is humorous, adding, "Nothing could ever substitute for the glory of beauty itself."

I recently had a rare phone call from Ruth. She was at an airport with her husband, Randy, off to a country, the name of which I couldn't quite make out amid the airport noise, to work on a commissioned painting. She didn't have much time, but I had the chance to ask her about the faith we shared so long ago. Her voice brightened as she replied, "God has been with me in all of my work! He shows me the way. I listen to Him and I can fail in a thousand ways and He gives me grace to go on."

Ruth signs her paintings, *"Your Artist, Ruth Mayer."* Her legacy will live for a thousand years and beyond.

"He has made everything beautiful in its time ….."
Ecc 3.11 RSV

What principles and values from this story are also foundational in your life?

From Ruth _____

_____

JAMES GIDEON ABERNATHY

Photo: Boaz Crawford

WHAT WILL YOUR LEGACY BE?

LIVING IN GOD'S WILL

As a boy, growing up in Cincinnati, Ohio, James Abernathy loved sports. His passion was to play major league baseball. Every other vision for the future was always a backup plan. Playing baseball under good coaching taught him a lot about life and how to develop the skills and character traits necessary for success later in life.

He says, "I had the blessing of the best coaching right at home. My dad was my coach most of my childhood and was the head coach of my summer baseball team the last five seasons I played. Playing sports, I learned how to develop the skills and character traits for success, no matter what you do in life."

James was raised by godly parents in a Christian home. He was given an early foundation based on the teachings of Jesus Christ. The family went to church on Sundays. He and his older brother spent summers running around the neighborhood with friends, checking in with the folks when it was time to eat. James had good friends at church and enjoyed participating in the church youth group.

He was a B average student who didn't do well in math, but excelled in social sciences and humanities. With supportive parents, he was sailing through school and sports. Just before the start of his sophomore year in high school, his life was to change forever.

It was just one of those things that teenagers do on a hot summer day. James went swimming in a friend's pool. They were playing

Marco Polo, a form of water tag. On a dive, he hit his head on the bottom of the pool and broke his neck (C-5 level). James became permanently paralyzed.

Immediately following the injury, James could not move anything below his neck. The neurosurgeon who performed his surgery said he knew right away from the x-rays that James would never walk again and informed his parents of that opinion within hours after the injury.

"My parents decided not to pass his prediction on to me at the time, James confides. "Of course, the doctor had no idea whether I would walk again, even though his expertise in the field could not be denied. God's power ensures that no man's plans or predictions are set in stone. However, over twenty years since the injury, I am paralyzed from my collarbone down and have limited use of my arms."

James offers this testimony:

"My faith provided the foundation for my perspective on life. It defines who I am. Humans can endure a great deal of suffering when that suffering is imbued with meaning. Suffering becomes extremely hard to bear when someone believes it is meaningless. Christ's suffering brought meaning to my own suffering and its role in the development of my character is making me into the man He created me to be.

"I thought God's will for my life was to go as far as my baseball skills would take me. I had no idea what God was doing, or would do, with me. My injury violently shifted my entire identity. However, God, in His infinite wisdom, began to show me, through other people and other victories in my new life, that He is at work and never abandoned me.

"One of those times occurred after the surgery when I was still doing therapy to regain what use of my body was returning as my body slowly healed. As I was slowly able to start using my biceps, I was able to, or should have been able to, use a splint on my hand to eat with on my own. But, seeing my own identity as forever stuck in needless weakness, I got used to other people feeding me and resisted when I needed to learn to do it myself.

"Then one night my parents and I were eating spaghetti at the dinner table. My dad refused to help feed me. My mom, although reluctant, also joined him. I sat there pouting for a while and refused to eat. Eventually, and it took some time, I ate the whole plate of spaghetti by myself. I still couldn't pick finger foods up to eat them, but I could use a fork to scoop. I've been feeding myself since that moment.

"I cannot imagine how difficult it was for my parents to do that.

"The importance of that moment cannot be underestimated. It meant that I would not spend the rest of my life with a victim mentality. Yes, I had limitations, but I learned it is unacceptable to use my disability as an excuse to rely on others when it is something I can do, or would be able to do with some hard work and faith."

"My faith is a blessing from God. It has been a dynamic faith, changing as my character and beliefs have been influenced by new understandings of Scripture and experience. It is the lens through which I interpret my experiences, contemplate truth and understand who I am.

"Meaningless suffering leads to bitterness, anger, depression, despair and hopelessness. Even through my roughest times, suffering enabled me to identify with a suffering Savior. Every believer has access to these truths. He is not ignorant of life's difficulties and has purposes for every one of them.

"I believe the Christian worldview provides a better interpretation of suffering than any other worldview. Two of my favorite verses are Romans 8:18 and 1 Peter 5:10. I also identify with Paul's writings on weakness, including 2 Corinthians 12. A story I identify with is the story of Gideon in the book of Judges. Gideon also happens to be my middle name."

With renewed resolve and determination, James graduated from Lakota East High School in 1998, graduated from Miami University (Ohio) in 2002 with a B.A. in Philosophy and Religion, graduated from Fuller Theological Seminary in 2005 with an M.A. in Theology, and graduated from Regent School of Law in 2010 with a J.D, ranking seventh in his law school class. He worked as in-house counsel for a small business in Southwest Ohio, primarily engaged in commercial litigation.

In the fall of 2014, a friend suggested James submit his resume to Talent Market for an opening for an attorney at a Northwest think and action tank in Olympia, Washington. James was interested but doubted it was possible for him to move across the country on his own, considering the amount of care he relies on. The recruiter suggested he give it a try. Once again, God did immeasurably more than James could imagine.

It was a good fit and today, James Gideon Abernathy is Litigation Counsel to the Freedom Foundation in Olympia, Washington. He's going to court and winning cases in a field he is passionate about and he is impacting the law and culture to promote liberty. That's exactly the kind of career James hoped for when he started law school.

He says, "I love going to court! It is the closest thing to game time in sports that you come across in the law. All of your preparation and practice come together and you have to deliver. One of the things I loved about sports is that you had to deliver when it counted. Of course I love winning and I hate losing. But as a believer, I know that God's kingdom goes beyond and through what humans consider winning and losing, success and failure.

"Looking back, I can see in my life where God's kingdom was furthered through, and even because of, moments in life that I considered a failure at the time. I am motivated by my view of work and what it means to be created in God's image – the *image dei* in each of us.

"After all, God works! He worked to create the universe and everything in it. He works through Divine intervention and performs a miraculous work every time someone is saved through the ultimate work of God, which was Christ's substitutionary death and resurrection. Whether it is a service, a widget or an idea, the outcome of work is creation. More than that, work is an act of creation within your own character – no matter the result.

"Barriers to work range from artificial rules and structures which discourage work and production, to a welfare system that encourages the absence of work, to economic policies which deprive humans of the ability to create wealth and create more opportunities for work and freedom, to workplace arrangements and coercive policies that crush the human spirit in those who wish to build, create and innovate.

"I go to work to free people from the chains of such coercive policies. God's kingdom infuses all things with meaning and purpose. This includes work, along with the unique skills and talents every human possesses, which should be used in a believer's service to the Lord and His kingdom."

James fits right into the camaraderie of the brilliant staff at the Freedom Foundation. His dedication to hard work, his facile mind and legal skills are a tribute to his can-do attitude. His wry sense of humor makes heavy work light. His boss, CEO Tom McCabe, says "James Abernathy is full of life! He does everything with great enthusiasm and passion. His legal briefs and courtroom arguments are always memorable because they are filled with devotion and zeal. James believes in fighting for those less fortunate who cannot fight for themselves. He is funny, irreverent at times, and always a joy to be with."

There is a delightful irony in James' journey from young, promising baseball player, to permanent paralysis, to an esteemed academic record and a successful career in law. God has brought him full circle and given him a new identity in Christ. James says it's the one He had planned all along.

"I consider that the sufferings of this present time are not worth comparing with the glory that is to be revealed in us" Rom 8.18 RSV

What principles and values from this story are also foundational in your life?

From James _____

_____

LTC GREG MAHONEY'S OFFICIAL RETIREMENT
May 2010 and the Legion of Merit award for 22
years of distinguished military service.

WHAT WILL YOUR LEGACY BE?

AN AMERICAN HERO

*"The Founding Fathers entrusted liberty to us. We
have the solemn responsibility to sustain it, promote
it and secure it for future generations. America is
on the right side of history as long as it continues to
uphold the principles of its founding."*

Gregory S. Mahoney, LTC, USA (Ret.)

Americans remember all those who gave their lives for the cause of freedom. And we lament the fact that so many veterans come back from war with mental or physical injuries that change their lives forever.

Greg Mahoney knows about such sacrifice.

Greg is an American hero who served his country with honor for nearly 23 years. His remarkable career began with a three-year ROTC scholarship after which he was named a Distinguished Military Graduate with a Bachelor of Science degree from Loyola University of Chicago in 1987 and entered active duty as an Army 2nd Lieutenant.

He says, "What a reality check it was for someone fresh out of school, used to the comforts of his Midwestern home and now serving as part of the most dangerous board game the world has ever played – the Cold War – between two superpowers with potential to destroy civilization. For the first time, I realized how precarious the world can be."

While stationed in West Germany, global events took an unexpected turn and Greg deployed to Southwest Asia where he encountered the stark hardships that many people face in our world.

"It was there I came to know that *charity* knows no artificial or political boundary, even in the midst of human upheaval. I will never forget the poor woman, clad in long, black garb, standing in the middle of an arid desert. She approached a group of us who were wearing the world's most intimidating military gear, holding out to us a basket of fresh tomatoes and smiling in a gentle gesture of friendship and gratitude."

This and other encounters left an indelible impression and Greg decided he had to do more. He returned to the States to train as a Special Forces officer and in 1992 was awarded the coveted Green Beret. He served assignments in the Far East, Europe and in our embassies abroad, mainly in former east bloc countries.

In 1996, Greg met his future wife, Doreen, an active duty naval officer studying for her Master's degree while Greg was at the Defense Language Institute. They married in April 1999. In 2000, Greg earned a Master of International Affairs in Security Policy and Russian Studies at Columbia University. Their first son, Sean, was born in 2001.

Juggling two different service requirements, Army and Navy, the family struggled with separations. Greg was in command of a Special Forces Company in Colorado and Doreen was a Navy Base Executive Officer in Virginia with their little son. The toughest separation for the couple came when his unit deployed to Northern Iraq in March 2003 where his Company conducted missions in Dahuk, Mosul, Kirkuk, Tikrit and other locations north of Baghdad.

"I have to tell you. Greg says, "that domestic turbulence pales in comparison to the numerous heroic acts of courage and selfless service that I witnessed on the part of our great American military in Iraq."

During Operation Iraqi Freedom, on August 28, 2003, Greg became one of those selfless heroes we remember every Veteran's Day. Here is his heartrending story:

"In the midst of the Iraqi insurgency, my team was caught in a vehicular ambush. A bullet to my right shoulder damaged all of the nerve cords and the artery in my right arm. Flown immediately to Germany where my wife joined me, I was then evacuated to the States and Walter Reed Medical Center. I awoke September 6 from a medically-induced coma. I don't recall much about the ambush, but am thankful that no one on my team was killed. By the grace of God, I pulled through and began the long road to recovery."

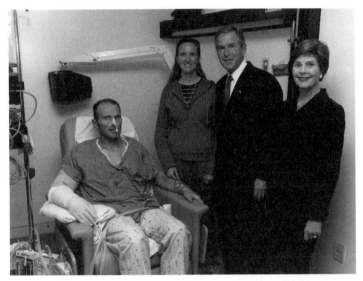

Greg, just out of surgery, with Doreen and
President and Mrs. George W. Bush by his side.

His right arm paralyzed, Greg underwent therapy to keep the tendons and muscles flexible and healthy until the nerves had a chance to regenerate the entire length of the arm. He battled scar tissue formation in injured areas, and in the nerve canal, greatly slowing the progress of regeneration.

"The doctors worked for two years, trying to secure the best possible outcome for me. My right hand took the brunt of the injury, so I do not have the fine motor skills. The psychological impact of the slow recovery was frustrating, to say the least. Loving support from my family made the challenge easier."

For his injuries, Greg was awarded the Purple Heart Medal which was pinned on by President George W. Bush at a ceremony at Walter Reed.

In early 2004, Doreen and Greg were reassigned to the Pentagon and his therapy continued for two more years. Their second son, Clifton, was born in Virginia in 2005.

Greg worked at the Pentagon six years, in policy for the Assistant Secretary of Defense for Special Operations and in Operations for the Joint Chiefs of Staff. His last assignment was as Deputy Division Chief, USCENTCOM Division, in the Regional Operations Directorate, where his days were filled with all of the operations ongoing in the Middle East.

He adds, "I retired in May 2010 mainly due to my injuries sustained in Iraq. Doreen, a Navy Commander, had retired a few months earlier. We didn't want to separate our family again with future assignments. I had served my country well and wanted to make a difference in a new way."

Doreen and Greg Mahoney with sons,
Sean and Clifton

Son, Sean is now 15 and will start his sophomore year in high school in Seattle. He is excited about his school and is on the JV football team. Clifton is 11 and will start 6th grade. He loves swimming and soccer and even tried cross country. Both boys are Scouts and are on track to earn Eagle Scout.

After military retirement, the family moved away from the beltway in DC to spend more time together and become more engaged in our local community. "We wanted to go where the outdoors would be beautiful, the boys would have good schools and there would be good prospects for future employment," Greg says. "Since we both had lived in the Northwest before we were married, we decided to settle in Washington state where both of us got involved in volunteer work with our church, school and community.

Greg is candid about retirement: "Sometimes it seemed as though we had never stopped working full time. But we receive many blessings in return. Doreen now teaches a Robotics enrichment course, and spends a good amount of time shuttling the boys around to various events, accompanying me on Knights of Columbus functions and helping our Boy Scout troop. I serve as a Scout leader in the Cub Scout program. The entire family volunteers and serves various roles in our church, St. Joseph Parish."

Greg was elected to a state officer position for the Washington State Council Knights of Columbus in May 2015, and reelected in May 2016, one of five elected state officers. Together, they manage and lead over 17,000 Knights and 163 Councils in Washington State. As a state officer, Greg is also a member of the Board of Directors for two major charitable funds in the Washington State Council. He was hired in October 2015 as the parish business administrator at St. Monica Parish on Mercer Island, WA.

Greg is concerned for America:

"As I see it, what is happening in our great country is the same trend that has visited many powerful civilizations in human history. Civilizations that have lost their way through political incompetence, corruption, selfishness and by rejection of the natural order of the world in which they have been placed. And, particularly, when a society loses its focus on Divine Providence and tries to become its own master and source of moral, spiritual and legal truth, this becomes the telltale condition that will usher in societal decline and certain collapse. All one needs to do is to look at the ancient empires of Egypt, Rome, Carthage, Persia, and more recently the states of Nazi Germany, Imperial Japan and the Soviet Union.

"But, we can change course before it's too late, by returning to the principles our Founding Fathers entrusted to us – those principles that are so eloquently enshrined in the Declaration of Independence and the Constitution of the United States – both of which acknowledge our singular dependence on God's good grace to preserve life, liberty and the pursuit of happiness. When we follow those principles and live lives genuine to fundamental truth, only then will we get ourselves out of the downward spiral of today's irresponsible secular culture.

"We need to reject the 'me' culture, the culture of death, the culture of relativism, the culture of political correctness, the culture of self-worth and self-determination. I would suggest the way to do this is to commit oneself to the ideal of service to God and to one another. This means we need to commit to reality – to truth. We must also forcefully confront the opponents to truth who intend to do us harm through terrorism, conventional war or other nefarious means.

"Lastly, we need righteous leaders TO LEAD. We in return should demand accountability, and respond swiftly to any abuse of power and position. Double standards in accountability are a recipe for disaster and dissent. Just take a look at the current mess in our federal and local governments – a total abomination of leadership. This has got to change.

"We have been entrusted with the greatest Republic this world has ever known. Some of the biggest threats to the preservation of our way of life are: 1) Stripping God out of our society. By separating church and state, our Founders never intended to remove God from all public discourse. 2) The blurring of right and wrong. 3) Technology, as great as it is, threatens to replace our mental ability to think through problems. 4) The ridiculous notion that we are entitled to everything just because we exist.

"The need to educate and empower others regarding the issues of our time is what drew us to support conservative public policy organizations. I am hooked on their noble missions."

> *"If my people who are called by my name humble themselves and pray and seek my face, and turn from their wicked ways, then I will hear from heaven, and will forgive their sin and heal their land."* II Chr 7.14 RSV

What principles and values from this story are also foundational in your life?

From Greg _____

_____

MARILYN IN TREATMENT

SURVIVING CANCER

Marilyn's Story

Life was good. We were "retired," secure, kids out & productive, grandkids to play with & spoil. My husband had recovered from quadruple heart by-pass surgery in 2011. The only cloud was a sick dog.

In early October, 2012 a journey began that took over our lives. My husband noticed what he suspected was a lump in my left breast. We were scheduled to take our dog, Bonnie, for diagnosis and surgery on her leg at Washington State University Wednesday, October 10-12 of the upcoming week and I decided to wait until we got back to check out the possible lump. I rationalized that I had had a clean mammogram just six months prior so a week or so it wouldn't hurt..... right?? Let's get the dog situation out of the way before we start the next thing.

Bonnie's surgery had a successful outcome.

October 18th I saw the OB/Gyn. She wasn't sure it was anything but just to be sure, ordered a mammogram. Two days later I was referred to a different place for a re-take. I laid there, waiting for the read. The radiologist came to talk to me. Why was the radiologist here?? She was sorry to say it looked suspicious.

Fear flooded through me, my heart sank, my lips quivered as I tried to stifle tears that were starting to well up. I drove home in shock feeling my life had suddenly become an unknown. I walked into the house and broke down, sobbing in my husband's arms. Then came the determination that we would attack this together and we would win!! That became our total focus.

The whirlwind started. Biopsy: yes, infiltrating, lobular breast cancer. Next decision: where and to whom to go for treatment. We chose Overlake Hospital – smaller, closer, no bridge to cross. We consulted others. It turned out to be the right decision for us.

On October 24th, we met our caring, yet direct, no-nonsense surgeon. She took over our calendar: MRI, CAT scan, meet the oncologist and the radiologist. An MRI-guided biopsy on other breast showed a small lump. Surgery was set for Nov. 7th. From pictures and tests, the initial thought was we were working with a Stage 2 cancer, but nothing would be certain until after surgery.

The oncologist had two possible treatments, one more aggressive than the other. At this point, he was thinking the lesser one would be fine. He went through the prognosis and survival rate statistics of surgery alone versus adding chemotherapy versus both chemo & radiation. Then he stressed I was not going to be a statistic. There was no hesitation. We would do it all.

Next big decision: reconstructive surgery or not. This needed to be decided before surgery. After consult and advice from a plastic surgeon, we decided against reconstruction. With radiation, I was advised that my skin would lose its elasticity and it would involve another major surgery in my case.

The radical mastectomy was performed Nov. 7th, exactly three weeks from the time I saw the OB/Gyn. Surgery went well. BUT the cancer wasn't Stage 2; it was Stage 3C, just a breath away from Stage 4. The lump measured three centimeters. The cancer had already advanced into my lymph nodes. Of the 18 lymph nodes removed, 16 had metastatic cancer. Thus I stand steeped in gratitude for my husband's discovery. If not for him, I am certain it wouldn't have taken long for this cancer to have metastasized to other parts of my body, greatly diminishing my survival chances. I asked the oncologist to revise the survival chart for my new diagnosis of Stage 3C. He said he wouldn't do it, repeating again that I was not going to be a statistic.

The Cancer team at Overlake Hospital felt that due to my general good health and physical condition, they would be "aggressive." After four weeks of healing, another minor surgery was done to place the infusion port and chemo was started. The chemo regimen was four times of two drugs at two-week intervals, followed by eight weekly treatments with Taxol.

I didn't feel good, but was blessed with minimal nausea. Instead I was famished. I was up at all hours eating peanut butter and jelly sandwiches. I lost my hair, was tired, you could see the effect of the drugs in my discolored/thickened fingers & toenails. The tiredness and recuperation time took longer and longer after each treatment as the killing of my body accumulated. The last chemo treatment was March 20, 2013.

During chemo, I was grateful for the recommendation to do physical therapy to try to return maximum stretch and flexibility to my arm movement. It hurt.... and as chemo progressed, sometimes it took sheer willpower to go...... but now I am blessed to have good movement which apparently some survivors do not.

One more hiccup occurred. At my appointment to be mapped for radiation, the nurse & doctor noted I had an irregular heartbeat. But I felt fine! They finished the mapping, rechecked my pulse and called for an EKG. I was pronounced in Atrial Fibrillation.

Great! Oh, please, God, not something else! Staff immediately called for a wheelchair and wheeled me to the ER. I had no knowledge I was in A-Fib, except you could see my heart rate jumping all over the place on the monitor. After four hours, they had started to prepare me to be jolted with paddles to convert me to a normal rhythm.

At the last moment, as the cardiologist was doing a last sonogram, she said "wait, wait....I think she's trying to convert". I believe the thought of having to swallow an ultrasound device to check for blood clotting in my atrium and the call for the paddles, shocked me out of it. The upshot? Now a cardiologist was added to the mix and blood thinner was to be added to my regimen.

On April 9, 2013, radiation started. My schedule was five times a week for 33 times. Again, I got progressively more tired as treatment continued. The painful burns took weeks to heal. But my hair had started to grow back!! ..... though it continues to this day to be thinner and more sparse.

My husband not only discovered the lump, but was there by my side every step of the way. We are private people and our desire was to "do it ourselves," so largely it was just the two of us. He was at every doctor visit throughout, every chemo infusion, every radiation burn treatment. He drove me to physical therapy, he helped treat my radiation burn and wrapped me up, he even took over the housework (ala hired a housekeeper). We were in this together – two determined people focused on the goal of beating the cancer.

I'm a fighter. There was no sitting down and asking "why me?" It was more "why NOT me? What was so special about me that I be spared from something so many other women had to fight? I had enjoyed good health for 68 years. There was no time to waste. Let's get started and beat this! I researched and talked to people. I kept a positive attitude.

I prayed every day, every night. And I accepted God's will for me. I did wake up a few times in the middle of the night, fearful, scared. And my husband held me in his arms. I asked for prayers from everyone, including the author of this book. Those special women, the Carmelite nuns, were praying for me. I trusted whatever happened to me was in God's plan. I was just going to try my hardest to cooperate.

While I was in chemo and my immunity was low, I skipped Sunday Mass, but I put on my soft, warm skull cap and would go to daily Mass when I could during the week, sitting removed, but participating. God was with me and I trusted He would give me the grace and strength to get through this time.

I received flowers and encouragement from family and friends. There were lots of cards throughout the months. I was astonished that so many cared. I felt the strength of their support, concern and prayers. They buoyed my spirit. I was encouraged by others who had gone through this and felt a genuine sisterhood with them. I was not alone in this fight.

The team of competent, superb doctors and nurses who cared for me made a huge difference. They were positive, cheerful, reassuring all the time. We actually looked forward to infusion time because of the rapport with the staff and the friendships we developed with other patients. The camaraderie was so encouraging!

I've gained a new sense of my mortality and learned that life is fragile. How much time do I really have? It gave me impetus to re-evaluate my priorities. Previously, I was more worried about other people's happiness and needs than my own; stressing, worrying, constantly on the run, always busy doing or fixing. Now I have no choice but to seriously take care of myself if I want to survive and keep future cancer chances at bay.

Marilyn today

Photo: Alpha 1

It's a work in progress, this unlearning of a lifetime of habits. I need to learn that everything doesn't have to be perfect, nor do I have to do it all. We kept the housekeeper. I keep reminding myself that getting enough sleep is essential to my well- being. I have trouble implementing that. My intent is to take time to do things I enjoy, like playing the piano and tap dancing. I'm getting better at saying "no" and trying to look out for myself. I have a ways to go. When the chips are down, what's really important comes into focus.

Wonderfully, my self-image has not suffered from the loss of my breast. I am very accepting of the new me. I am reassured by my husband who tells me I am beautiful just as I am, and that what I am missing doesn't matter.

Am I courageous? No. Exceptional? No. Just determined to make it and grateful to God for His healing mercies.

> *"I can do all things through Christ, who strengthens me."* Phil 4.13 RSV

What principles and values from this story are also foundational in your life?

From Marilyn _____

_____

From Dave _____

_____

BILL AND MARILYN CONNER

Photo: Joel Sorrell

WHAT WILL YOUR LEGACY BE?

A LEGACY OF PARTNERSHIP

Coming together is a beginning;
keeping together is progress;
working together is success.

Henry Ford

Bill and Marilyn Conner exemplify the word "partnership."
Together, this extraordinary couple has met the challenges
of their business and personal life to achieve high honors and
a legion of devoted friends.

Behind Bill's understated demeanor is a rare strength of character
and perseverance that helped him to advance the political processes
that affected the homebuilding industry as he led his company,
Conner Homes, to leadership in the field. Those traits have also
helped him through some very difficult times. Winston Churchill's
famous words about never giving in have been Bill's guide. Marilyn's
courageous leadership at home and with the family business is the
perfect complement to Bill's strength.

Giving in, giving up, would have been the easy thing to do in
the first decade of Bill and Marilyn's 61-year marriage, but it never
occurred to them! After earning his degree in Civil Engineering
from the University of Washington in 1953, Bill went to work for

Morrison-Knudsen Company on an Air Force base in Mountain Home, Idaho. There he met Marilyn, whose dad also worked for M-K on the base.

Their courtship was interrupted when Bill finished that project and left for another job. Marilyn says, "He kept driving up from Boise to see me, and mother wouldn't let him stay in our house unless we were engaged, not even on the couch. Dad liked Bill a lot. Mom didn't want me to marry anyone in construction because she knew it was a hard life. I figured if I wanted to keep him, I'd better marry him. Bill sent mom a big bouquet of roses. He even built her a porch. She softened and approved our marriage."

The Conner's started from scratch, moving from state to state, working in heavy construction. "We went where the jobs were," said Marilyn. But, after five years, two little ones and living in a mobile home, we decided to join Bill's brother, John, in the residential development business in Seattle. John ran the office and managed financing and architectural plans. Bill supervised the construction work. I landscaped the lots to help sell the houses. I wallpapered, too – even upside down because I didn't know better. Both of our children worked sweeping out houses, raking rocks. There was no free lunch. Everybody had to earn their keep."

The hard work began to pay off. In 1973, shortly after the 1970 Boeing crash, brother John retired, and Bill continued on his own as Conner Development Company. He became active in builder organizations, and through this work, helped advance the political processes that affect the industry. Bill says it came as a shock to him "to find that there were actually Socialists in the state legislature."

As the Conner's prospered, so did their service to the community. Bill and Marilyn made many lasting friendships along the way. One friend asked Bill to contribute to an endowed professorship at the University of Washington Medical School. He ended up helping to fund one chair in diabetes and then another in cardiology.

Bill says. "It wasn't easy at the time but we did it and learned a valuable lesson we've never forgotten; that when you give money away, you don't miss it because it comes back."

"I don't think it does any good to get angry about the needs of the community and do nothing about it," Marilyn adds. "It's nice to help public policy organizations that you trust are looking out, not only for your interest, but everybody's interest, especially in the example of good government. I don't have time to understand every issue which makes issues like vetting political candidates very important."

Marilyn founded the Friends of Alzheimer's organization at the University of Washington about 25 years ago. Under her creative direction, the annual auction became a highly anticipated event, bringing in much needed funds. She is well known for her ability to bring friends together for good causes.

The Conner philanthropy extends to a number of charitable organizations in Mexico and Somalia. "Education is our passion," Marilyn says. "In Mexico, school ends at sixth grade, and children need help to go beyond that and have a chance to succeed. We help with extra things like back packs filled with school supplies. We support five children by buying their uniforms, shoes, gym clothes and bus fare plus a small stipend. This encourages parents to keep the kids in school. A few of these kids are our friends even today."

Bill and Marilyn went with a group on a round-the-world-trip and, while visiting Mali, learned that only 16 percent of the girls and 32 percent of the boys were literate. So, on the plane coming back, Bill and one of the other men went down each aisle, selling a program to support girls education in Mali and a medical clinic in Buhtan. They landed with contributions of $8,000 for each.

In Seattle, the Conner Foundation at Holy Names Academy supplies scholarships for inner city kids. Bill's philosophy is that education is the whole foundation of the democratic system. "If you have uneducated people, they will take the word of the best fast-talker and elect him to office. We also need competition in education here in Washington state. Without competition in schools, you don't have excellence. The money should go where parents and kids want it to go."

Bill Conner, a man of humble beginnings, has walked with presidents. He speaks reverently of President Reagan as "just a regular guy like the rest of us, but a great man who believed with all his heart in freedom."

"We need freedom!' exclaims Bill. "We need to support those organizations that stand for freedom and honesty and transparency in government. We have to keep after government, especially in this state. For example, decades ago, the first plat of land we built on was 110 lots, and we got it processed in six months. The last one took about five years and a lot more money. There are so many expensive regulations, it is very difficult even to get into the business now. It squeezes out the entrepreneur.

"Nobody manages the regulators. They think we are *their* public servants! Small business needs support. They see the problems every day.

"I have provided a useful product for people. I never wanted to build high-end mansions. I support policies that fight for *everybody,* for you and me and the neighbors to have good lives. I learned a lot from my folks. You work for a living, treat everybody fairly and honestly and you have discipline in your life.

"When I was a young boy, my dad was gone all week. He would leave me with a list of chores and paid me 50 cents an hour. One weekend, he didn't give me a list and he came home and said, 'Bill, what do I owe you?' And I said 'nothing.' He asked 'Why?' I said 'because you didn't give me a list.' My dad said 'You KNOW what to do!' I never needed to get another list and I got paid every week."

Bill says he's glad to have been born during the Great Depression because he learned so many life lessons. He is concerned but hopeful about the future of our state and nation. He says, "Democracy doesn't change until it hurts. There has to be some pain involved before people see the light of change and which direction to go. I say open your eyes. Keep them open because things change all the time. That's what we have always told our kids."

When asked about what he is most proud, Bill is quick to say, "the kids and the business!" His son, Charlie, started working with his dad in the sixth grade and is now the owner and President of Conner Homes Company. Marilyn adds, "Charlie bought the company in 2000 and did a very good job. Then the crash of 2007 hit all of the homebuilders very hard. Charlie worked his heart out to save Conner Homes and we did what we could to help with financing. The 'too big to fail banks' left the homebuilders out to dry but the small banks stayed with Charlie.

"It was a very stressful two years for all of us, but we were well rewarded with Charlie's determination and grit. Bill and I hope that, with a pro-business government in place, all small businesses will do better so that individual business owners will not be stifled by heavy regulation."

Both of the Conner daughters are successful, accomplished married women and have presented Bill and Marilyn with five grandchildren. The close family was jolted by the terrible news that granddaughter Sarah had been diagnosed with cancer at age 17. Sarah lived five years after her diagnosis, was able to graduate from high school and attend Stanford University for two years.

Grandpa Bill's eyes glisten when he talks about needing Winston Churchill's reinforcing advice for such a time as this. "Never surrender to cancer or to anything!" he says. "If you have a problem, you try to solve it and you have faith it will turn out all right." It is so hard to see your children suffer," Marilyn explains. "Going through this tragedy has made me more spiritual. It has changed what I think is important. If you don't have family and friends and faith, you don't have very much."

> *"Never give in, never give in, never, never, never, never – in nothing, great or small, large or petty – never give in except to convictions of honor and good sense."* Winston Churchill

What principles and values from this story are also foundational in your life?

From Bill _____

From Marilyn _____

FORMER U.S. REPRESENTATIVE, LINDA SMITH

SAVING ONE LIFE AT A TIME

I n 1998, after more than a decade representing Washington State in the House and in the United States Congress, Representative Linda Smith accepted a phone call that would completely change her life. The caller was Mr. David Grant, a missions director for the Assemblies of God in south Asia – a man she had never met, but he had heard Linda speak at an international convention.

She listened for forty minutes in speechless shock as he talked with great passion about girls kept in cages, women living literally as slaves in degradation and imprisonment and other truths about the despicable sex trafficking business which has become a global disgrace. Mr. Grant implored her to come to India and see for herself.

Linda felt real trepidation but, at the same time, felt compelled to make the trip as soon as her calendar could clear.

She landed in the middle of the night at Bombay Airport and was asked where she wanted to go. Responding simply that she wanted to see what she came to see, the men with Mr. Grant looked at her quizzically. Linda persisted having been told that brothels conduct most of their business at night.

They took her to Falkland Road. What happened, in Linda's own words:

"A 13-year-old girl crouched in a dark corner on the dusty floor, her hair dirty and tangled, her eyes hollow and lifeless. Raw sewage flowed through an uncovered ditch on the other side of the thin brothel wall.

The scent of a hundred men clung to her small frame. Her expression revealed total desperation. This look was not 'Please help me." This was a look that said, 'I am doomed forever, beyond help, beyond hope.'

"It was as if God Himself whispered in my ear, *'Touch her for Me.'* My hand suddenly weighed 90 pounds. I froze. My head felt light from holding my breath. I could taste the stench. Would I contract a deadly disease by just breathing the air? But I could not ignore the internal voice, *'Touch her for Me.'*

"Obediently, I reached out and touched her dirty, frail shoulder. In that moment, my life changed. At my soft touch, the desperate little girl fell into my arms with gratitude and I felt her heart beat against mine. My simple gesture shocked her because she was so utterly unloved in this world.

"Suddenly, the stench evaporated. She didn't appear filthy. She appeared beautiful. She was not worthless! She was a child of God. I raised my tear-filled eyes to look around the small room. Dozens of girls sat around me – all trapped in the same living horror as the instruments of India's sex trade – slaves locked in cage-like conditions, existing to satisfy the sexual appetites of the next man wanting to buy them.

"A man entered the room. He tapped a girl on her shoulder, summoning her to service another man. She followed obediently. This time, my stomach roiled, not with stench, but with rage. *Who could do this to a child?*

"Falkland Road in Bombay is one of the worst brothel districts in the world. I passed hundreds of stalls along the narrow street, each containing dozens of girls, each one sold by her owner to 20 to 40 men per day.

"How could I return to the safe halls of Congress as a U.S. Representative knowing this little girl and thousands like her live every day with the fear of beatings, starvation and rape? These were just school-aged girls who had been sold into slavery by desperate parents, or abducted and spirited away by masters of the sex slave industry.

"I had to do something!"

That was almost twenty years ago. Linda Smith left her life in public policy and founded Shared Hope International, a non-profit organization with a mission to lead a worldwide effort to eradicate the marketplace of sexual slavery ... one life at a time. Linda, like so many of us, has walked a healing journey of her own. Rather than allowing her past to define her, she has turned it into a catalyst to come alongside others on their own path to healing.

Shared Hope, International is headquartered in Vancouver, Washington with a second office in Virginia. Its mission is threefold:

To PREVENT: *(no one should be in sexual slavery)*

To RESTORE: *(every victim deserves a chance to be free and to heal)*

To BRING JUSTICE *(laws and public policies must protect the innocent and punish the perpetrators).*

One of the first projects undertaken by Shared Hope International was creating two Villages of Hope: Ashagram north of Mumbai, India, and Asha Nepal, near Kathmandu. "Asha" comes from the Sanskrit word for "hope." In these safe environments, young women who have been trafficked domestically or in neighboring India, have the opportunity to rebuild their lives with their children. The villages also serve as a haven for children who have been orphaned in one way or another, as the result of their mothers being sold.

Linda Smith with Manisha and Pooja

Manisha and Pooja are two girls who were rescued and restored by God through the work of Shared Hope International.

Manisha came to live in Asha Nepal after the age of seven. Her mother, who grew up very poor, fell in love at the age of 16. The man offered her a job and a better life in the city.

"But she was betrayed and sold in India," Manisha tells in her story. "She was soon pregnant with me, but did not want a baby because a boy was destined to be a criminal and a girl, a sex slave like her. She started to neglect me.

"That's when my dear Aunty, also trafficked to the same brothel as my mother, began to take care of me. But neither one was able to save me until the wonderful day my Aunty was rescued by the team from Bombay Teen Challenge. She urged my mother to let her take me with her, to seek shelter there, but my mother was not convinced. Instead, she sent me to a relative in Nepal.

"Later, my Aunty came to Nepal and searched for me. When she found me, I was miserable. The relatives used me as anything for money. I am told I lived there for three years. Aunty immediately arranged to bring me to Asha Nepal. Asha Nepal gave me the parental love and care I had never had. They gave me a family! The best part is, I know Jesus. I was living in a dark cage, but He used people to rescue and restore me. I believe that God had a plan for me from the beginning and He allowed these things so I could testify that He is the one true God!"

Today, Manisha has graduated from college with a degree in Social Work and plans to bring change to her country by helping restore trafficking victims back into society, where they can live full, joyful lives. Linda had the joy of returning to Nepal in March of 2016 to celebrate Manisha's wedding.

Linda at Manisha's wedding, March 2016

Pooja was 8 when her mother fled with her to Asha Nepal. Here is her story:

"My mother was the eldest of seven," says Pooja. "When her father died, she and her mother raised the younger children. At 16, my mom married and soon I was born. When I was five months old, my dad married another woman for her dowry and left us without food or money.

"Mother desperately struggled to care for me, but life was hard. I was very sickly. Just to survive, she left me with my father and his mother and returned to her own mother. Then a woman offered her a good job in a Kathmandu factory. That woman's 'sister' arranged the trip and gave my mom some dry meat. It was drugged. She awoke as a slave, thousands of miles away in a Mumbai brothel, where she spent five miserable years in pain and darkness, without hope.

"Meanwhile, I was in severe distress. My cruel stepmother forced me to do all the housework and take care of my stepbrother. I had no education, proper food or clothes. I could not remember what my mother looked like.

"My mom was finally rescued by the team from Bombay Teen Challenge and went to Nepal to stay with my Aunty at Asha Nepal. They formed a plan for rescuing me. When she came to my village, my stepmother hid me. She wanted to keep her slave. But one day, my mom grabbed me and we ran!

"We fled to Asha Nepal. There I got everything I had been denied, a good education, food, clothes, and lots of love and care.

"At age 9, I accepted Christ as my Savior. All of my painful experiences have helped me realize that God is there for me. Jeremiah 29:11 became real to me. I know that God has a good plan for my life; whatever He does is to prosper me; to give me hope and a future.

"I will graduate with a degree in Business Administration to become a banker and build my own business. I want to glorify God and encourage women who have gone through the same pain my mom and I experienced. I believe that God will help me achieve those dreams."

In its nearly two decades of operation, Shared Hope International has created models for long-term homes of restoration in India, Nepal, Jamaica, and South Africa, as well as in other countries, and partners with other groups and organizations who are also committed to restoring the lives of victims of sex trafficking worldwide. More recently, Shared Hope International has spearheaded an effort in the United States to ensure that no minor is further victimized by the judicial system by being criminalized for crimes committed against them by pimps, traffickers, or buyers.

In the Smith home, the commitment to create a world in which sex trafficking no longer exists isn't limited to Linda; her husband Vern helped form *The Defenders USA, the Men of Shared Hope,* after hearing an FBI agent testify about the alarming increase in the number of men watching Internet porn, which was increasingly becoming more violent and using younger and younger girls. It became clear to him that day that what is so often seen as a women's issue is in reality a men's issue.

The Defenders USA, the Men of Shared Hope, is a brotherhood of men who have pledged to stand against the dangers created by the commercialized sex industry here in the United States, which, more often than most care to admit, preys on youth and children. Together with Shared Hope International, *The Defenders USA* co-created a training resource in 2016 that equips churches and other places of worship with the tools needed to protect the children in their own congregations and communities from predators. Bottom line, according to Vern, if men don't buy porn or sex, the demand for women and children being sold as sexual commodities disappears.

Though actual numbers may be higher, it's estimated that 100,000 children are being bought and sold for sex in US cities and towns on a daily basis. For Linda and those working alongside her, Shared Hope International is more than a cause. It's a pledge to protect our children and to demand justice for those who have been victimized by sex trafficking.

"If you hold back from rescuing those taken away to death, those who go staggering to the slaughter, if you say, 'look, we did not know this,' does not he who weighs the heart perceive it? Does not he who keeps watch over your soul know it? And will he not repay all according to their deeds?" Prov 24. 11,12 RSV

What principles and values from this story are also foundational in your life?

From Linda _____

_____

From Vern _____

_____

From Manisha and Pooja _____

_____

MARY JO AND C.J. KAHLER

A HUMANITARIAN LEGACY

E very Tuesday for 16 years, Mary Jo Kahler has driven 58 miles round trip to volunteer at The Pediatric Interim Care Center in Kent, Washington. PICC receives at-risk newborn babies from nearly twenty hospitals throughout the state; fragile newborns who have been exposed to drugs during their mothers' pregnancy and require special care as they go through withdrawal sometimes from as many as five different drugs during their development in utero.

PICC had its origins in the late 1990's as a vision of two foster moms who saw a growing need for specialized drug withdrawal treatment among the foster babies they were caring for in their homes.

Center Director Barbara Drennen says, "We are kept very busy providing immediate, short-term medical care for the babies in addition to educational support services to the community in the management of substance abused children. We continue to see a rise in Heroin use reflected in the babies we serve. Their toxicity levels and the amount of support they are requiring indicate that the potency of Heroin in our area is becoming strong. Heroin is not the only drug in their systems. Most are also exposed to methamphetamine, methadone and prescription drugs.

"Last year, we admitted 86 babies with 71 of them positive for two to four drugs in their systems. We saved the state $1,699,340 last year by caring for babies who weren't quite ready for home care, but didn't need to stay in the hospital." It is not a coincidence that PICC is located just a block and a half from a police station.

Mary Jo shows up to go to work. Some days, she is a "cuddler," meaning that she holds babies, giving them a loving, caring human touch. Other days, she handles multiple loads of laundry, restocks shelves, and otherwise helps out wherever she can. When items are donated to the Center that they can't use, Mary Jo loads them up in her SUV and delivers them to a local baby and children's nonprofit group which works with social workers from throughout the region who have needs for their clients and children newborn to 12 years of age.

She learned about PICC watching a local television feature story on the Center and was touched by the compassion of the director and the mission of the nonprofit organization. Mary Jo says, "Children are my passion. I had been saying for some time that I wanted to help an organization whose mission statement matched my values – even if they just needed their toilets scrubbed so that their dollars could go directly to care for the babies. I am honored to be a trusted member of their team in whatever way they need me."

Mary Jo's altruistic nature and love for children are well known throughout her state going back to 1970. That was the year Washington state became the first in the nation to legalize abortion by the vote of its citizens. She says, "I was pregnant with our third child and very aware of the life growing within me. I could not stand silently by while a child's life would be legally, arbitrarily and intentionally ended in a nation whose very Constitution affirms an innocent individual's right to life. As I felt my daughter moving inside me, I knew she was alive. I could NOT deny her humanity and that's what I would be doing if I failed to try to stop the killing that was ahead if Referendum 20 passed."

Mary Jo joined the opposition team, *Voice for the Unborn*, piled her two young kids into her Datsun B210 and distributed literature throughout her County. Sadly, the Referendum passed. As a result, her life changed forever.

In 1971, a former professor she highly respected from her college classes at Seattle University, offered Mary Jo the opportunity to speak for the *Right to Life* position as a member of the newly-formed board of directors of *Human Life of Washington*. Soon after she accepted that role, she was asked to also take on the chairmanship of the group's state speakers bureau. In the years that followed, numerous other states asked Mary Jo to help them set up similar speakers bureaus for them. The goal was always to educate, not agitate. She says, "You don't lose when verifiable truth is on your side."

Mary Jo became the pro-life voice on television, radio and print media, countering the message of speakers from Planned Parenthood, NARAL and the Death with Dignity lobby. In 1987, she became the Executive Director of Human Life of Washington.

By 1992, the life issues of unlimited abortion and euthanasia became the subjects of ballot initiatives in her state. All of the organizations that believed in the individual's Right to Life knew that they had to fight these measures. So Human Life's board brought leaders from these pro-life groups together at its office to strategize how best to respond.

By the end of the long meeting, Mary Jo was asked to direct the effort against Initiatives 119 and 120. Initiative 119 was an attempt to legalize assisted suicide, the so-called "Death with Dignity" Initiative.

On election night, what had seemed nearly impossible less than a year earlier, became a never-to-be-forgotten vindication. Voters heard the message against Initiative 119 and sent it down to defeat! The surprise of the evening came on Initiative 120 which proposed to expand on the right to abortion that had been state law since 1970. On the final count, Initiative 120 passed by less than one half of one per cent – the equivalent of one vote per precinct in Seattle/King County.

Mary Jo resigned her role as Human Life's Executive Director but remained engaged until 2000.

Paralleling Mary Jo's pro-life work, her husband of 53 years, CJ, a registered pharmacist in Washington State, led the Washington State Pharmacists' Association in its efforts to oppose the position of the Washington State Board of Pharmacy that pharmacies have a duty to dispense all lawfully prescribed drugs including medications designed to provide emergency contraception. These medicines were also referred to as the "morning after pill", which in some situations may act as an abortifacient. This position of the Board was being taken in spite of the US Constitutional First Amendment rights of free exercise of a citizen's religious beliefs.

CJ was the first pharmacist to stand against the Board on this issue that was a very long battle that went all the way to the United States Supreme Court. The High Court eventually decided not to take up the Stormans v. Wiesman case in Washington state, citing that "the government designed its law for the primary, if not sole purpose of targeting religious health care providers," essentially upholding the trial court's finding.

In the late '70s, CJ and Mary Jo teamed up for another principled fight, this time in the education arena. When they learned that three members of the local School Board had violated the Washington State Open Public Meetings Act, they joined with four other sets of parents in the District to hold the board members accountable in a Recall election. CJ served on the leadership team and Mary Jo used her pro-life messaging skills to oversee all written and verbal communications to ensure the integrity and accuracy of the charges they had filed.

She says, "We wanted to be able to look our kids directly in the eye with our heads held high." The three board members were recalled by the voters, the first time such an action had been successful in the State.

Eight years ago, Mary Jo heard about a group called "The Soup Ladies" and decided to become part of their team. Founded by a woman who owns a restaurant and is also the Chaplain for her local Fire Department, the team prepares food in advance and in times of crisis serves hot nutritious meals to law enforcement, fire and search and rescue workers when they are called out on a long mission. A few guys, dubbed "The Soup Gents," are available to help with the heavy lifting.

Mary Jo says, "We all have food handlers' permits and have taken classes for emergency response certification. The group has a canopied pickup truck that is stocked at all times and ready to go, as well as a mobile kitchen trailer for those times when we are on extended missions. The team has its own freezer, donated by CJ's Rotary Club.

We are always prepared to respond to a call from an Incident Commander and be out the door, ready to feed a hot meal to 100 people within one hour. We are humbled to be able to give back to those men and women who give so much to make our communities safer on a moment's notice."

Mary Jo reveals her personal philosophy of helping others:

"I believe in a loving God who gives each one of us unique talents, not just for our own betterment, but for the betterment of the human family. It's a responsibility. I can't solve all of the problems of this world or this country, so I use my time and treasure in ways that can actually make a difference in the human condition. At my core, I am a results-oriented woman. I want to enable people to move out of their circumstances so they can be, in whatever way they choose, a positive, contributing member of the human family. I believe we can all be examples of God's love to our world, in our own unique way."

This dedicated humanitarian couple is engaged in many other meaningful activities, but they say that none of their "titles" are as meaningful to them personally as "Mom, Dad, Grandma and Grandpa." Their three grown and successful children are the happily married parents of their six grandkids and thoroughly enjoy family gatherings together.

> *"Truly, I say to you, as you did it to one of the least of these my brethren, you did it to me."* Mt 25.40 RSV

Irene M. Endicott

What principles and values from this story are also foundational in your life?

From Mary Jo _____

_____

From CJ _____

_____

JEREMY JAMES ENDICOTT

WHAT WILL YOUR LEGACY BE?

A FIERCE FAITH IN GOD

Jeremy's story, as written by his little sister, Amy

C hurch Sunday School was finally over!
We flew home, threw our stuff in a bag, and left for an afternoon of swimming at a nearby lake with friends. We passed our parents on the way out exchanging quick hellos, 'where are you going,' and goodbyes.

Windows down. Wind in our hair. Singing with our friends at the top of our lungs! It was a good day. A beautiful day. But a day that quickly turned into a nightmare.

Later that afternoon, on August 9th 1998, we drove away from the lake with one less person.

My brother Jeremy was a typical 18 year old kid. He was stubborn, adventurous, and teased me about boys. After all, I was his younger sister. He was involved in soccer, advanced classes, theater, and church youth group.

Jeremy was also good with the ladies, which now makes me smile but back then it just made me gag. He once convinced his friends to serenade a girl at her front door so she'd go to the prom with him. So yes, he was brave too.

His bravery extended to the stage as witnessed in July 1998 as he and a friend sang a duet in church. The song, now very dear to us, was *Beauty for Ashes* by Crystal Lewis. We have the tape of him singing the lyrics "He gives beauty for ashes, strength for fear, gladness for

223

mourning, strength for despair…- words that we would so desperately need to hear a few short weeks later - and in his strong voice no less.

Singing was a creative expression from Jeremy. He was also a deep thinker as revealed in his poetry, fiction writing, and personal journaling. But what I love about Jeremy is that, in addition to a dig-deep intention, he was playfully adventurous.

Earlier that summer, stricken with boredom, we engaged in an epic pillow fight that resulted in accidentally putting a hole in the wall. We wrote our last will and testimonies that day, certain our parents would punish us mercilessly. We may have fought hard as siblings but we laughed hard too.

Despite the relentless challenges and dramas of being a teenager, Jeremy genuinely pursued God and tried to live in a way that pleased Him. He created a secret bank account to stash money aside for people in need. He was popular but befriended peers who were a little rough around the edges. (Which reminds me of the time a motley neighborhood boy knocked on Jeremy's window in the middle of the night, needing a friend, only to scare the living daylights out of my aunt who was staying in Jeremy's room while visiting.)

Jeremy had the crazy ability to bridge being an athlete *and* a thespian; popular *and* approachable. It certainly was unique for his age.

Jeremy was no saint. He was not perfect, as I well know. But Jeremy was undeniably smart, compassionate, intentional, kind and witty.

So many reasons to miss him.

On that afternoon of August 9th, 1998, Jeremy and his friends went swimming across a channel of the lake while I stayed on shore. After hearing splashing and commotion I walked to the bank to see Jeremy struggling to stay above the water as a friend tried to help him. Despite being close to shore, he was in deep water. I yelled for him to float on his back and relax to regain strength. He tried but he was too exhausted.

As Jeremy slipped beneath the water one last time, I watched his air bubbles break on the surface and began to scream.

A little over an hour later we sat in the back of an ambulance, his body in a yellow plastic bag laid between me and my parents who had arrived after receiving my frantic phone call. Eventually we signed his death certificate sitting on the curb of the parking lot. We found his shoes and t-shirt still sitting on shore, put them in the trunk of our car and drove home in agonizing silence and shock.

Where were you, God?

In the days, weeks, and years that followed, my family faced a difficult but critical decision: Believe God is sovereign or believe He is not. Our journeys to the answer were different; different timelines and different grieving, but we all arrived at the same answer.

Yes. God is sovereign.

He is mighty to save but He did *not* save Jeremy. We can't comprehend why until we join him in Heaven, but God is still good.

As believers in Jesus Christ, we have the blessed assurance of Heaven and its sweet reunions. We lean on God's promises of peace, purpose and love while leaning into the unpredictable waves of doubt, anger, and helplessness that ebb and flow in the grief journey. Through our pain we still recognize God's kindness toward us.

Less than 24 hours after Jeremy died, my parents sat on our backyard swing begging God for a symbol or sign that Jeremy was okay in His Presence. Out of a desperate need for peace, my father asked to see a deer as a simple symbol. And not before they could walk back into the house, there was a deer in the yard. A fawn.

Every day that first week there were deer in our yard. And at the lake on a few of our annual trips out to remember Jeremy. And in the orchard behind me on my wedding day as we exchanged our vows, there were deer. God, in His great love, has sent us deer as a symbol of hope and peace, sweetened by the fact that one of Jeremy's favorite songs that he'd play on the piano was "As the deer panteth for the water so my soul longeth after You..."

Jeremy and his little sister, Amy

When you lose a loved one, life can become simple. You make the most of what you have and take nothing for granted. The grit and messiness of life eventually catches up, all too easily, but you have sobering moments of perspective because you live in the harsh reality that life is fragile. You're compelled to make life count; to leave a legacy.

Legacy. It's such a wildly meaningful word to us.

At Jeremy's memorial service, we offered people an opportunity to share stories about him. We heard so many new stories and details of his life (like the time he got pulled over by a cop – a detail he never mentioned to us). Although all the stories were beautiful, it was the words of his high school principal that captured so perfectly Jeremy's legacy: *"A fierce faith in God."*

You can find these words etched into his headstone on a grassy hill in our town of Newberg, Oregon. If you were to venture here, you'd find a small tattered oak box tucked behind his headstone. Inside is a pen and a precious journal filled with letters, prayers, lamentations, and stories; all intended to remember and honor Jeremy. It's become a safe place for friends, family and even strangers to share raw, unedited emotions as we continue our journeys here on earth. Eighteen years and seven journals later, Jeremy's legacy of kindness and faith continues.

It's not lost on us that one day we, too, will have a headstone. What would be written in our graveside journals?

What do you think would be written in yours?

> *"He reached from on high, he took me, he drew me out of many waters… He brought me forth into a broad place; he delivered me, because he delighted in me."*
>
> Ps 18:16,19 RSV

What principles and values from this story are also foundational in your life?

From Jeremy _____

_____

From Amy _____

_____

EPILOGUE

Dear Reader,

My hope in bringing you these heart-touching, inspirational true stories is that you might see in them some of the very principles and values that you practice in your own life and that will be part of your legacy. Could you relate to any of the lives you read about? To the bravery and courage of Mel Nesteby; the stewardship of the Starkenburgs; the joy and caring of Terrie O'Neal; the obedience of the Sundquists; the dedication of Bob and Jane Williams and the responses as God helped Marilyn survive traumatic illness; and James' triumph over disability, just as He did for Bill Weitzel; does your marriage resemble the marriage of Dana and Brent? Would you give up the good life for a great cause as did Linda Smith and do you have a fierce faith in God as Jeremy surely did?

I encourage you, now that you have finished this book, to look back through the book and complete your own written principles and values from each story that you can relate to your own life. Use the lines provided. *Then, one day, give this book to your children.*

I encourage you to re-examine your life, however young or old you are, and ask God's help if you recognize that some changes might be made. God can show you a new pathway to leaving a legacy that will be recalled and honored by your loved ones for generations.

I am one who had to learn the truth that God never leaves us as we are. He wants us to grow in wisdom as the years go by. Take time to look back over the years of your life. See if you don't recognize God at work, in the good times and the bad. See the blessings you didn't see then. That's growth. That's opening the door to change.

Three grown daughters went to lunch following their father's graveside service. There was small talk about their young families, sharing of recent photos and promises to get together more often. Then, one of them broke a silence, saying "I'm going to miss Dad." The second one nodded her head in silence. The third one waited a beat, then said, "Who was Dad?"

Was he absent? Was he a workaholic? How does it happen that three sisters did not have a clear understanding of who their dad was?

My prayer for you is that no one in your family will ever say, *"Who was Dad?"* or *"Who was Mom?"* May you be involved in your loved ones' lives. Tell them who you are, what you believe in, what you stand strong for and your hopes and dreams for their lives. Always and often, let your children know you love them.

May you have the courage to fix a broken relationship, to apologize for wrongdoing or to confront with love and forgiveness for someone who has wronged you. Healthy change can happen when you recognize that it is needed before it is too late.

Change can bring a new beginning of a better life and better relationships. The relationship to begin with is a personal relationship with Jesus Christ.

May God bless you and may you build a lasting legacy story for those you love and who love you.

Irene

NOTES

1. The ArrowHead: Winning the Story War, by Kevan Kjar
2. KidsTown, International: www.kidstown.org
3. FrontSight Military Outreach: www.frontsightmo.org
4. Family Policy Institute of Washington: info@fpiw.org
5. Life history of Peter W. Schramm by Dr. Christopher Flannery, co-founder, The Claremont Institute. Learn more about Peter Schramm: ashbrook.org/peterwschramm
6. History and art images provided by Randy Holden, Ruth's husband and Artist Manager; www.ruthmayer.com
7. Shared Hope, International: www.sharedhope.org
8. Excerpts and photos courtesy Sgt. Reece Lodder, Marine Corps Recruit Depot, Parris Island: *Remembering Greeley*; www.marines.mil/
9. Mission House: www.missionhouseministry.org/
10. Pediatric Interim Care Center: www.pic.net
11. Joel Sorrell: *Sorrell Design & Photography*, Joel@sorrelldp.com
12. Boaz Crawford: *This is Artistry, LLC*, thisisartistry1@gmail.com
13. Freedom Foundation: www.freedomfoundation.com

Irene encourages you to contact her: iefreedom@wavecable.com